D1613026

WRITERS REPUBLIC

HOURGLASS
SOCIOECONOMICS
GLOBAL INTERPRETATION

THE BRIDGE BETWEEN WORLDS
VOL.3

BLAINE STEWART

WRITERS REPUBLIC L.L.C.
515 Summit Ave. Unit R1
Union City, NJ 07087, USA

Website: *www.writersrepublic.com*
Hotline: *1-877-656-6838*
Email: *info@writersrepublic.com*

Ordering Information:
Quantity sales. Special discounts are available on quantity purchases by corporations, associations, and others. For details, contact the publisher at the address above.

Library of Congress Control Number:		2021912439	
ISBN-13:	978-1-63728-501-5	[Paperback Edition]	
	978-1-63728-502-2	[Hardback Edition]	
	978-1-64620-844-9	[Digital Edition]	

Rev. date: 06/16/2021

Preface

The Golden Gate Bridge was built to connect land masses and ease the travel burden of workers commuting into the west coast city of San Francisco. Besides its functionality, the Golden Gate Bridge symbolizes the final gateway that opens and closes our effort in manifest destiny, expansion west, and journey through the perceived final frontier. We all know the final frontier is to the stars and then much further, but our journey to the launch pad must come first. Barriers of land and sea combined with topographic changes in elevation must be crossed to reach our final destination. The symbolism of a massive steel and iron expansion across an open body of water is clear that nothing can come between humanity's ability to engineer solutions to the inevitable problems Earth provides. Whether it is only a mile wide or thousands of miles of the open sea, there is always a way.

The Bay Bridge, south of the Golden Gate, serves the same purpose as a ferry system of boats from the East Bay. Suboceanic or a subway that goes under the bay into the city is the same as a transoceanic flight from New York to Paris. Engineering marvels and capacity for technology to solve problematic conditions are no different when we speak in terms of advancement toward a universal collective goal. In simple terms, if we had an equation where $1 + x = 2$, a technological solution, whether elaborate or simple, holds the same value as $x = 1$. The massively complex equations that determine an airplane's ability to stay in the air at this point are irrelevant. Our goal is to do whatever it takes to sum all solutions in this simple equation that balances x to equal 1. Where cementing foundations securely in the ocean floor and then expansions secured with wire to suspend a massive platform for transportation is complex, the combined value is simple toward our common goal. Tunneling into and under the bay is difficult; indeed, it is a simple solution in balancing our equation.

The truth we find in elaborating the complexities in this way of simplicity is to understand there has not been one form of land or sea mass we have not been able to traverse and connect. The world and systems we know as cities and countries are then connected not by space but by time. Sure, we cannot walk to London, but we can call someone there. We cannot swim to Australia, but we can buy a plane ticket. We cannot drive our car to Japan, but we could hypothetically drive our car onto a massive ship, and that ship will take our car there. As we pull our car onto a ferry, we are frozen in space. It is time that transports us toward another field state in the vector of space. If the world were to remain disconnected, at this point, it is not by distance but the loss of time in our transformative transportation to and from, whether physically, ideologically, or communicatively. As we move from field state A to field state B, it is now not the width of our funnel but the width of all funnels as they cohesively bond systems together at each edge and flow as one sum of all molecules down a stream. As a bridge does not necessarily have to expand across the ocean or bay, a stream or river is sufficient in our analogy, just as a natural bridge could connect the rabbit and deer population if one habitat is relatively placed on one side or the other. But, just as a bridge can connect the lion and gazelle population. The critical factor is the point to which habitats and people are connected and where. Are we bound by ideology, law and justice, commerce, or are all of these factors working against our cohesiveness?

Introduction

Hourglass Volume 3's effort is to lay the framework through global interpretation to explain the state of affairs through the past, present, and then predictability of what is to happen into the future. We must understand in a very cliche way "where we have come, so we know where we are going." Our analysis in this volume is just that. The past tells us our future and the exponential and measurable rate of cohesive properties or gravitation toward instability. You can probably guess already just by your interpretation of the world around you. Sure, not as many countries use barbarism to govern, but a more insidious system may be in place. It is easy to see evil in bloodshed but hard to see in white-collar monetary transactions and non-exposed injustices, and genetic prejudice. Slavery does not exist the same as what we fought against in the Civil War, but it could live in a different elemental state. Where the clear wrong was apparent and sides and lines are drawn, insidious tactics spin the form of understanding. The increased cognitive ability of both friends and foes further pit one against the other. Where wrongs can be seen, they can be unseen but still present. In this sense, a confederate soldier could be tricked into fighting for a cause with an effect they do not see in a true light, only partial. This is the current state of affairs.

The goal is not to spin some insane conspiracy but very rigidly explain the relationship between entities in measuring cohesiveness that avoids absolution and pulls toward global field state zero. There are hundreds, if not thousands, of foundational cracks and faults throughout the world but also thousands of positive reinforcements. We will isolate the most commonly known and interpreted and measure the cohesiveness based on ideology, the strength of commerce, and the type of authority and government in respective countries. The structural foundations of cohesively connected entities are essential. There is a measurement of cohesiveness between nations, among every country, and even minutely between government and globally recognized individuals. Meaning as someone in the vastness of a socioeconomic vector of space, I am a variable to a transient living deep in the Siberian wilderness. However, I have never been there and don't know who they may be, but we are connected by the Earth. We breathe oxygen from the same supply. We consume the same hydrogen particles from a stream after one molecular combination rises and falls from the sky. In time, we are not divided nor disconnected. In space, we are.

Because tension does exist as a default product of friction as a measurement of relativity, we'll have both positive and negative charges of cohesiveness. The world is a dark place but not absent of light, and perhaps that perception shapes the world we live in. The world is not dark but bright. It is not that we have darkness as a product and component of the universe. It is only that our light is not bright enough to sustain its power and positivity. Sometimes the world dims that light and it flickers, but it does maintain a current of electrical charge. The strength of our light, or its flickering surge, is determined by the measurable perception in how we look at the relationship between parties and what point of reference we see the world. Like an arbitrator or mediator, an unbiased eye will shed light where a biased mind will miss the mark. Our goal is to look through the lens of every perception in this volume as we study and interpret motive and polarity.

The first lens we'll look through is the party or entity that sees the effect of an action and bounce from perceptions of cause and effect. For some cases, this is both or all parties, but that is irrelevant. Our interpretation is not one entity or another but the perception of an affected party. We look at the entity that places a cause in motion, link a motive between, and shape reasonable logic to corroborate an effect. What causes a country or two countries to go to war? What is the impact of war, and what does the world see? When human nature and corrupted reasoning are a force involved, how does a third party perspective view the motive and logic behind an event? How do internal variables within that entity act as a funnel vortex leading to transformational and transitive output? How does Hitler convince a nation and create a nationalist army? On the other side of the spectrum, how does Martin Luther King affect a country and the cascading effect from perspective viewpoints? What brought input that created output? For example, how does slavery in the US lead to a higher cognitive understanding of social issues or further abandonment of justice? How does Shakespeare and the Renaissance ultimately shape our understanding of the arts, literature, cognitive ability, and awareness as a whole, and then how is it manipulated? Just as the spark ignites a fire and a caveman has warmth, how can we look at the cascading evolution of society through historical events that shape the past into the present that affect our future? The perceptive ability of human nature and interpretation set the stage for the individual as a part of the whole as a body of water cohesively flows down a stream.

What we do and what occurs through time will always be seen on a spiritual level. The simplification of this balancing ebb and flow of positive and negative transitionary principles between and among entities is the war between good and evil. The challenging part is who decides what is which and which is what. The natural individual believes they know all they can understand and that anything they cannot contemplate must not exist. Because we have difficulty admitting we are wrong, the world is as it is by natural design. The law of averages and a vast collection of individuals adds to this. I can write this book because I will always believe I only understand 1% of knowledge that exists in the universe. Even with every word and new understanding, that percentage will never increase, but the total capacity of 100% will. I am only one person. As the world goes by and the universe expands, 1% then is pretty good relative to an infinitely vast universe of space and time.

I can say this because I have been wrong and know I will continue to be wrong if I make an assumption based on incomplete data. Who then, as the question stands, decides good and evil? The truth? No one. The pure terms in polarity chase into infinity and oblivion. Why? Evil is never in the interpreter, only the interpretation where "good" is found only relative to our ego. Sure they are "good" but can't be as "good" as me, right? Just as the expansion of collective cognitive ability is not instant, progress is naturally met with defiance. That is just how we are. If not, we would solve every human or engineering problem instantaneously. The natural thought process is the same as just above. "That is impossible because I have not thought of it." No, it is possible because anything is possible in a universe of infinite possibilities. We are just limited in our effort, by human nature, to accept personal faults by design. At first, we thought we would never travel to the moon, but before that we thought with absolute certainty the Earth was the center of the universe because naturally, we are enveloped in our own understanding. Before that, the sun was just "bright" and didn't have a name.

To be clear, we are not at the center of the universe. We are the universe. Not only were we wrong once, but twice until we were right and then wrong again. We made it to the moon but never would we go to Mars. Some random dude from South Africa living on the West Coast disagrees. We are not evil for this. However, we tend to gravitate toward the same point, but we use a less scary word than evil, simply being "wrong" more than we are right. However, rights add up as a sum more substantial than all wrongs, just as light is not the absence of darkness, but darkness is the absence of light and can fill any dark void without prejudice. If not, the world itself would already have fallen into absolution. This process of logic is the number one fundamental flaw that makes the world what it is today.

A small grouping of individuals absent of this trait has the same if not more power than a large group of individuals with it. If an army fights with evil intent and arrows against nuclear warheads, the effectiveness of modern science over pointy sticks is apparent. One person with a warhead against a million fighters with simplistic weaponry has the upper hand. In the same way, countries grouped act against or for one another based on the ability or inability to take, process, and accept or deny new information. It is not so much what that information is but a willingness to listen to understand instead of listening to respond. Mostly response is an act of aggression, whether fiscally or physically.

Wars have been fought, and populations lost to the insidiousness of misunderstanding. At the same time, what warrants the use of a warhead if those you are at odds with are incapacitated from understanding the cause to use one with the burning effect well known? Is it the lesser of two evils we accept or, the greater of two goods we want to strive for?

The choice is simple. When you choose one lesser evil at one point in time, the next option presents a more dangerous lesser evil until you get to the bottom of the barrel. The same inverted choice ladder then exists on the opposite side of the spectrum. The choice of peace can lead to a greater choice of peace if the commitment to it remains. The danger then resides just as mentioned. A small group of people with power but absent of legitimacy or good-natured intent can sway the bond between all nations and prevent the goodwill of large groups of people. Vice versus the good will and intent of one powerful person can be delegitimized based on cognitive inability to understand the natural purpose of an action solely because they do not see why that surely exists. So the balancing act continues between good and evil, but perhaps one love does exist to delete the paradox altogether.

In the measurement of good and evil, we look at the perspective through current and past events that weigh against the state of affairs. On a spectrum of right and wrong or good and evil, how is an act perceived to both or multiple parties? Hiroshima and Nagasaki are terrible for Japan's country but good from the perspective of the United States in ending the pacific front of WWII. Winners write history, and we see details of the radioactive fallout absent from the drop and lost in time. Just as one can be "good but not as good as me," one can be "bad but not as bad as them." An atomic bomb kills hundreds of thousands but is justifiable by "at least this" or "at least that."

The United States capital insurrection is "bad," but the argument is it was not as "bad" as the burning of businesses during riots and protests. Again the fault in logic described in Volume 2 is present in this interpretation at the individual level. Then the process of understanding is found in the current global state of affairs we describe in this volume. Just as the duality basis for political dichotomy exists and affects the population within the United States, this polarity hedged approach affects how we see the world and how the world sees us. The spectrum of black and white is insufficient in measuring the beauty of the natural world. Beauty, as they say, is in the eye of the beholder, where it can be born anomalously in a dark room or the light. As we will find, the truth is that the measurement of light is irrelevant; instead, a relatively accelerated rate of filling any void is measurably desired. All of these questions, thoughts, and interpretations, and more, are the reasons for the following chapters.

We start from Medieval times and accelerate to the present day in laying a framework for further global field state analysis. Modern historical events interpreted include WWII and the United States and its Allies and relationships between Russia, Germany, China and Japan and the US before and after the war as a peak and placeholder more than actual direct analysis. The Cold War and Cuban Missile Crisis as global tensions mounted along the linear spectrum of communism and freedom. Iraq as the epicenter of conflict in the Middle East and perceptual involvement of the United States and cascading effects on European Nations and events on US soil. The current tension of North and South Korea following the Korean War, internal conflict within the continent of Africa, Europe and the Middle East and all other events by two or more parties, in history, can be analyzed through this universal lens.

Present-day ebbs and flows of hostility in the South Pacific. Directly in measure, Africa as a state in constant struggle for balance through the 19th and 20th centuries through proxy involvement. Iran, Saudi Arabia, and India in the fight for dominance along southern Middle Eastern resource lines. The axis of nuclear and economic superpowers of China, the US, and Russia affects smaller countries and regions. It seems like a lot of terrible relationships, but there is good in the world. Positive charges are discussed as commerce involvement across the globe through collective effort, though maybe un-optimized, trade agreements, and economic collaboration. The analysis of intercontinental collaborative effort is how these unions benefit the overall population, how long they last or lasted, and if they faltered where tension and friction break desirable cohesiveness. Obvious trade agreements include NAFTA, trade agreements through the establishment of the European Union, and trading prowess balancing between China and the US. As the self-proclaimed but likely legitimate number one superpower, our final analysis looks into the United States' involvement down to individual citizens of other countries across the entire globe entangled in a casual relationship.

Mr. Caveman's Global Expansion: Good, Bad and How?

Through the Vortex, Volume 2 re-introduced the caveman analogy as our starting point of growth into humanity and the natural ingenuity we have today. The characteristics of limited consciousness and cognitive ability, as our starting point, show exponential growth of understanding is a genetically encoded trait. But is this trait a good or bad thing? We know based on the studies of nature versus nurture, both factor into who a person becomes. On a larger scale, that then determines what the world becomes as a collection of individuals. There is no separation between the science of relationships between two people or all people, just an additional layer of complexity. You may simply compare A to B between two people. You perhaps add a few x's or y's and z's and natural logs, imaginary values, or exponents to measure this complexity, but balance and polarity are still present.

Nurturing something has its effect upon the cause nature presents. Opportunity or lack of opportunity will inevitably affect a decision that is made. A drug addict that uses drugs while pregnant impacts the genetic makeup of their child negatively. Once that child is born, nature is for the child to have similar addictive personality tendencies as the mother. But, what we don't think of in this sense is that drug use while pregnant is a form of negatively impactful nurturing that directly manipulates the natural makeup of the child.

Our caveman analogy is very similar. We must determine if our genetic makeup is the deciding factor as a clock's inevitable tick into time for something to grow. Or is the space we inhabit the dominant trait. Concerning the scientific process, let's add hypotheses and some deductive reasoning to situational challenges. If the first caveman to evolve was born without sight, how likely would he have been able to not only survive but learn without the assistance of a partner and discover fire? In another scenario, if the first caveman was perfectly capable by their genetic makeup but never met another caveman, how likely would it be that he or she invented the wheel and created further use of this new invention? In this scenario, there are hundreds of cavemen that exist but never meet and hold the same IQ and natural survival ability.

What would happen to the population in the effort of growth and expansion of understanding the world around? A third scenario is, what would a cave dweller do if they evolved on a planet that required nothing and gave nothing? Meaning, say there are no defining characteristics of each cave dweller's space to determine or cause cognitive growth? If a baron planet absent of plants, animals, or celestial bodies above were the caveman's habitat, what would contribute to their growth? Let's dive into these separately below.

Caveman Scenario One

Scenario one presents a problem for the first evolved caveman because he cannot see. For his or her survival, what is needed? He surely cannot hunt, for an archer needs their eyes. He surely can't build a shelter because a builder needs to find, discover or invent new tools. He surely cannot know what night or day is because the sounds of the Earth are the same regardless of light or absence of it. He can't wonder about the bright light in the sky that gives life to the plants and trees he trips over and runs into. What, again, is needed for survival? The nurture of another. A blind cave dweller can eat if another brings them food. The blind caveman can be sheltered from a storm if another brings them to a cave. The blind caveman can wonder about night and day if another explains when it is time to sleep. For the survival of our blind caveman, nurture is the dominant trait for survival and growth of understanding. Genetically, a blind caveman is absent of one integral attribute that nurturing can replace. Though more nurturing is required because of the absence of sight, the weighted importance of nurturing is higher than that of the absent ability to see where life can continue at a higher probable rate of living to procreate and even expand an understanding of the world.

Caveman Scenario Two

Scenario two presents a problematic situation where individual cave dwellers exist and act alone, with the same ability, but in isolation. In this scenario, let's focus on what the Earth gives but also takes and think of 3 different cavemen named A, B, and C:

Caveman A lives deep in the forest, relying on hunting and drinking from a small stream. By this time, genetic makeup has assigned survival traits to understand what hunger and food are and the natural and basic knowledge that water is needed to be consumed for survival. One windy and hot day, while walking down to the stream, caveman A sees a dark cloud in the sky that cracks a tree near him. A lightning bolt created a large wildfire the caveman had never seen. As the wildfire roared through the habitat, other animals fled, but not all of them made it. The caveman's food supply had scampered off, but he found an elk that became trapped. A carcass burnt to a crisp remained a hungry caveman A consumed and realized that was pretty good. Because caveman A had never seen fire before, he began to wonder what it was based on the genetic makeup of the Earth. In this sense, with an exchange of input to output and adding to the caveman's wonder, Mother Earth, without awareness, nurtured the caveman.

Caveman B lives on the edge of the forest on a flat plane, absent from any cave for shelter and distant from any water source or food supply. Caveman B found the perfect spot near a stream to build a shelter out of fallen trees and limbs but had no way to transport his materials. Suddenly, a rock rolls down a small hillside and a small tree limb is carried by the rock a few feet but just enough time for caveman B to see the ease in effort of the rock transporting the limb. Caveman B grabs the small stone and begins to experiment and creates a wheel and small makeshift cart that allows him to transport his materials to the point near the food and water supply where he is to build his shelter. The question then presents itself. Was it the caveman's ability to think based on genetic characteristics about a wheel, or was it the Earth that showed him in a nurturing way? Based on low cognitive ability, similar to a caveman that is almost blind, the Earth hinted. Again, to fill the void of natural knowledge, nurture from the Earth was the dominant trait that allowed the caveman to solve his problem of lacking efficient transportation. It is likely, the journey back and forth from a food source and shelter added a variable that would have prevented and stunted caveman B's ability to grow because his focus was on survival. Once he created the wheel and a cart, caveman B can focus not only on the trip between points but optimize his time and space with personal and physical cultivation where a situational burden previously negated the time to cultivate.

Caveman C lives on a secluded island with tropical attributes such as palm trees and coconuts and a small and limited water supply. Caveman C can see the mainland across an expansion of ocean water. Caveman C's natural survival tendency recognizes saltwater cannot be consumed by this time, and he will die if he relies on the ocean for water. Caveman C's freshwater supply is running out as it hasn't rained in a few solar cycles, and he thinks only of survival and wonder of the mainland across the expansion of ocean water. It is not too far, but the caveman tries to walk there and realizes he cannot swim. After a windy day, he sees a small tree branch floating out into the sea, and again a sense of wonder amasses. Caveman C grabs a bunch of fallen tree branches and constructs a small raft.

After a few test failures, he finds he needs to hold all the tree branches together and engineers some simple rope, and heads out into the sea. Even though he is floating, the current takes him away from the mainland, and inevitably he ends up back on the island. At that point, he sees a fish in the water using its tail to maneuver and realizes he can use one tree branch to push against the current. The caveman sets out again and uses a branch as an ore and finally makes it to the mainland, where a freshwater supply allows him to survive and thrive. The difference between the previous two and the Earth's ability to nurture each cave dweller is the rate at which survival is threatened. In this scenario, the death of the caveman from natural thirst and dehydration was impending and approaching where he had no other choice but to adapt.

As mentioned by the scenario presented, the main problem is that Caveman A, B, and C never cross paths. Individual survival and slight cultivation increased each caveman's standard of living, but they never shared their inventions. Caveman A didn't invent fire but witnessed it and attempted to replicate it. Caveman B invented the wheel based on luxury and simplified how he transported materials that allowed time to focus on cultivating new abilities. Caveman C created a raft and ore system to transport himself along a body of water for survival by reaching a new resource. Combined?

Human ingenuity and then exponential cognitive cascading effects can nonchalantly take us across or under the Golden Gate Bridge. Apart? Each cave dweller lives their own lives, and the Golden Gate Bridge in 2021 is not even a thought. The measurement of cooperation for procreation physically is a necessity as well as cognitively. In 2021 we probably wouldn't have expanded to the Americas if A, B, and C did not cultivate their ideas together. The question then remains, are we who we are for our genetic makeup or nurturing tendencies of the Earth? If we think of A, B, and C as one caveman, we add more complex properties, but the sustenance is the same, survive and thrive. From Volume 2, cooperation through nurturing is our accelerant against our genetic makeup. Let us look at the third scenario and finalize our hypothesis into a solution.

Caveman Scenario Three

The third problematic scenario dictating growth by nature or nurture describes a situation where a caveman or group of cave dwellers inhabit a world absent of distinct characteristics. The development and survival of the caveman population are not reliant on the world around them. The caveman population and genetic makeup of the caveman do not require food, water, or any resource given by the earth for sustenance. Imagine the Earth is more like the moon but even more boring. There are no other plants or animals, or streams. The sun does not exist, nor do moons or stars. Light is present, but day and night do not exist. The Earth is a perfect ball in space. How then does a caveman learn?

They don't. Because the Earth does not test the caveman, they do not need to adapt. Because resources are not required to be consumed, resources don't need to exist. The genetic makeup of the caveman sustains each individual. The odd question here is then procreation and population growth. What is the process, and what is required to procreate in a world that offers nothing in itself for development? How would the caveman exist in the first place if adaptability and Darwinist evolution are not present, needed, or required?

The questions of this scenario are the most difficult to answer because we do not fully understand even a world that does give life but also takes it. If we were to imagine the caveman was created in this characteristically absent world, would they grow their understanding? The answer is no because nurture is not required, but the genetic properties of the caveman also do not then allow for the growth of cognitive ability. It is impossible to learn if there is nothing to learn from. It is impossible to write a book if you have never seen a book or a pen and paper.

It is impossible to learn to communicate if you can't describe the relative relationship between a tree or an ocean. You can't give a name to something that doesn't exist and ask another what their word for the color blue is if red is not present either. The importance of this analogy is imperative and very simple. Say the genetic makeup of the caveman in this scenario automatically gives them the mathematical solutions to all of mathematics and physics, but if you cannot see a star in the sky, how do you interpret and apply this understanding? Because learning is dependent on the nurturing ability of our world, our growth is dominated by the nurture of nature. Without any empirical data, knowledge relied on nature's effort without nurture is divisible by the collective as a whole. We mean that, based on assumption, genetically derived growth without the benefit of knowledge attained by a nurturing process is divided with every cell. If we lack nurturing, ability is divided into nothing which nothing is then produced if we do not learn from our environment. A pair of parents that magically make a child in a world or universe that is not coded for growth will divide their understanding if nothing else is added. That is what you see in the world today. When a group of individuals does not learn, their offspring do not add any understanding to the collective or even garner any further understanding above the capacity of each pair of parents of that individual. Why do I think this? Because I know this and the deductive process in reasoning agrees to which the scientific process is a product of this process itself.

The collective knowledge of the universe is only a multiplier of what the universe is willing to give just as a test to each cave dweller in the preceding scenarios. Nothing about utilizing the wheel is added to a caveman that only understands fire, and therefore the car engine you have in your vehicle today would not exist. As two cave "people" create offspring their offspring do not automatically understand fire as they are assigned to the population that only knows the wheel. To add to that individual's knowledge of the wheel and its utilization, something else needs to be added in a nurturing environment. If nothing or anything like a rock rolling down a hillside does not occur, then the imagination process and wonder we have encoded within is not triggered. There is no thought absent of the senses of taste, touch, sight, and smell. You cannot think of building a boat if the view of the mainland shore does not give you a sense of wonder and need to survive.

The hunger and taste tied to a fire cooking a carcass do not introduce you to how fire can cook your food if a lightning bolt does not cause a wildfire. A world absent of any definable characteristic adds nothing and leaves us in a vegetative state even if we are coded to understand everything that does exist. Our interpretation is based on what is interpreted and the presence of defining properties tied to what is to be construed, and reliance upon the process of thought behind it. We can see the color of a rainbow, but our cognitive ability to interpret its beauty is solely determined by it being present. We are coded to solve, but our genetic compound is useless and a waste of God's gift if we cannot observe the interpretation. Infinity multiplied by zero is still zero.

The critical distinction should be made that anything that is not within us that acts to manipulate our understanding is an act of nurture. This includes the natural habitat we live in and the people in our lives or our parent's ability to nurture us into who we are even as an extension of their natural being. Nature is everything we are born with and every cell in our body. We nurture others as well as nurture ourselves in a good or bad way. It is not nature that decides what we eat for breakfast but our trends and tendencies that link us to what foods we enjoy. Sure, the nature of our cultural background leans toward one appetite over another, but we are nurtured into it. An American born from two American parents in Spain will grow into a different palette of taste. The way we nurture our taste buds manipulates our genetic coding, and our children's appetite is different from our own. The purpose of our questions raised in our process of cognitive evolution is, "Is this a good or bad thing?"

As we look into the world in the following chapters and segments, we start here to understand how we have grown and what process causes individual and collective growth. We must look into the world to recognize our relationship with others and that the habitat we live in determines who we are based on the experiences we have is dominant over our natural genetic makeup. If genetics were the dominant trait of growth, this study would be irrelevant because our reactionary principles are non-determinant of what occurs to us or around us in the world we live in. Yes, our coding is essential, but just as a calculator is useless without entering a formula. A computer does nothing without a power cable. Is this good or bad? Well, it determines what type of virus protection software we have. If we do our homework or our nurturer programs a firewall that explains what is on both sides of the wall, this growth process is a good thing (usually, we only see one side.) If a trojan can get behind our borders, this is a terrible thing detrimental to ourselves as individuals and the world as a whole as a sum of individuals. Genetically, we are not simply born to see all dimensions the universe gives us to analyze each choice in our lives because each choice adds a new dimension.

It is up to us to nurture our understanding, so growth in a positive way is inevitable. The insidiousness of the Trojan metaphor is that we are unaware of the danger within our own knowledge because the nature of our genetic makeup is the hardware of our computer, where nurture is our software built over time. Your mouse and keyboard have no awareness of what a virus is, but understand what happens when your mouse doesn't work. Just as we have arms and legs like desktop monitors and computer tower fans, our minds and souls make everything work together and give life to our process. RAM and memory vary from one to another as the interconnection of all is a powerfully helpful but equally dangerous technological advancement. Cave dwellers evolved into modern-day humankind, starting with sticks and stones to count, some things happened in between, and now we have the World Wide Web. Our purpose is to look into the world to see where we are now and look into history to understand the present and know the future of what could and should occur to ensure our process of involvement remains cohesive and coherent. From there, predictability is possible. The Law of Averages and Regression Models

The Law of Averages

To find the mean of any group or subgroup of a measurable universe, we take the average measurement as a valid parameter. As we have used to find lower, middle and upper class thresholds in previous volumes, an average is essential when weighing an effect upon the collective. Here, we see the sum of all individual parts computed to study and consider constraints against the system. This volume's effort is to piece what groups and subgroups are used to understand the differentiation or regression from the desired path toward equilibrium. Further, we get into how we measure and weigh each subgroup against our linear equilibrium model and what we can do globally to ensure this gravitational pull remains. First, we must open the puzzle's box to see what is inside before piecing it together. Key terms in our measurements are characterized as the bullet points below. These purely mathematical products are segments of our model in a computational sense applied to the sectors of comparison described in the introduction above: a system of government, ideology, commerce strength, and more.

- Group and Subgroup
- Collective Universe
- Individual Characteristics
- Mean Average
- Regression From the Mean
- Regression From Subgroups
- Desirable Mean Equilibrium

Group and Subgroup

A statistical analysis of a population requires parameter measurements and defined characteristics within our measurable components. When you run a statistical analysis on the effectiveness of a vaccine, sometimes you need to have a placebo group and a real-dosed group. That is a simple example; as we get more complex in comparing the relationships between and among all global countries and entities, we have to construct parameter metrics and decide what we will measure. Because we are interested in investigating the strength of involvement and equally cohesive balancing or mutually beneficial and reciprocal growth, we must set our groups and subgroups as rigid as possible. Are we looking at countries or corporations? Are we looking at dominant political groups within a country as a collection of subgroups that affect the reciprocity entirely against another set of subgroups within a particular country? Does a political party in Germany influence the German government that directly or indirectly impacts the US political process? Does one subgroup envelope the entire group as a trojan manipulates our source code? The rigidity of our measurement must be defined before actual data metrics are added to compare and contrast the strength of involvement and invertibility.

The Collective Universe

Again, all groups and subgroups add to sum all individual parts to form the whole and form the collective universe. The purpose of this metric is to apply a measurement to our entire global structure to see as one human race how far or close we are to a state of equilibrium. The difficulty is in determining desirability. Because we cannot place a relative measurement on something that has never existed, how do we know if and when we are approaching equilibrium? It is much simpler than you may think. We have polar components that accelerate the involvement and invertibility of entities in positive or negative directions and the velocity rate attributed. It is not the general direction, but the constant speed and growth maintained as a system moves into a state of absolute cohesiveness. It is discussed more in utilizing the Mean

Average, but our collective universe's goal is to have this measurement to use. The collective universe is everyone living and every cognitive being within a socio-structure of input to output.

Individual Characteristics

The subgroup, group, or collective universe have characteristics that make them different from other measurement groups. If we look at party lines, the average number of democrats to republicans will decide the weighted swing along the spectrum from right to left for the entire collection. Individual characteristics act as determinant factors in our study as aspects of the entirety of the universe or down to the individual within a group. Ideology, type of government, separation or cohesion of church and state, supply and demand system, and cultural demographics, among a plethora of other characteristics, can swing our measurement. Individual features can be purely numerical such as income or purely demographic, where thought can create equity differentiation between and within groups. For example, without looking at any other demographic, equity dispersion can determine if a social production system is out of balance with reality and stretched by bias in the wrong direction. Very measurable.

On the other hand, race can depict a similar story by measuring different characteristics. Say we are looking back into civil rights or even as far back as the Civil War. A measurement of equity was given or taken based on the hue of a person's pigmentation, where wealth, value, and influence are solely determined on this factor. Even though not as easily measured based on a single data point as simple as a dollar, the effect is present to the cause. Imagine a country where the lack of colored pigmentation determined if you were a slave, and this country was parked right next to the United States border. Ideologies of what race is "superior" would create massive tension that inevitably affects the system of commerce between the two entities. Just because we can only see black and white, the gray area of understanding between these two countries creates unbalanced involvement and the threat of war is pre-heating.

Mean Average

Acting as a determinant outcome and desirable measurement and the gap between the mean average is the simple computation of all individuals within a group or subgroup. We hope and strive for a determinant outcome as we apply constraint principles against a structure. The group is measured as an average based on individual characteristics. The mean average uses measurable characteristics to compare groups against other groups of even weight min and max measurements against the standard of the whole. Imagine the world with a social measure of movement to or from equilibrium being drawn on a graph and displayed in holographic form to show progress or regression from the mean field state of zero differentiation. We have a central point and hope as two or more thresholds for absolution to measure the relative placement at any static moment, between ticks on a clock, as movement to or from.

As the world moves closer to cohesiveness among all races, creeds, and countries, our graph moves toward a central zero point. This as well explains not only the relationship of the world but between individual people. A mean average chart displays this orbit as we described the involvement and invertibility in comparing sectors in layers of cohesiveness. Newton's gravitational laws depict something very similar in the string between two points and the weight of one affecting another. A mean average graph then plots all individuals in their journey of life. It measures a regression from the mean during certain moments in time where emotion, life events, growth, and decay, among many other things, can plot our path to or away from ultimate and absolute truth or fallacy. The collection of all individuals within a group, subgroup, or the universe as a whole then determines at what rate that set or subset is centered just the same. As we break down individual characteristics to place measurement upon a set or subset, we can see where we are strong or weak in a global or personal sense as a group compared to another. If our mean average measures and recognizes a gravitational effect toward economic efficiency and legitimacy, we can focus on ideology if we are weak in our spiritual truth. Just as a country strong in doctrine but weak economically, a focus can be placed on an uplifting look to improve one characteristic as time is of the essence and should be focused on foundational cracks before building other luxury levels.

Regression from the Mean

Once a mean average has been established, the regression from it is an important measurement that can be found. Diving deeper into the usefulness of measuring parameters within a group regression indicates outliers and the span of cohesiveness within that group. A mean average with a higher rate of deterioration is useless. Why is that? For example, if our mean average of two people is 50 and one person is measured at 0, and one person is measured at 100, in whatever characteristic, the relative relationship between these two people is distant in respect to the mean. Ideally, an average between two people being 50 has both parties measured at 50, making the standard still 50. Cohesiveness or friction is created in inverted ways.

Cohesiveness is when groups are close to each other in understanding, irrelevant of the physical distance. Conflict is when they are far apart in reason but close in physical proximity relative to the difference in understanding, just like our *ABi* and *B ln e* states. As we mentioned the plot of individuals upon a graph in the section above, the plot points of individuals and characteristics applied for measurement will depict a scatterplot graph. Our scatterplot is a perfectly straight regression line in a perfect world along our desirable mean average overlapping a computed equilibrium. Even if the mean average of a scatterplot graph of a set is a straight line, that does not mean that the group is founded in truth. A perfectly linear scatterplot can exist but gravitate toward absolution and not equilibrium. It is that popular cliche to be careful following the crowd and don't be afraid to stand out as an individual if you know you are right and they are wrong.

Regression from Subgroups

Just as a scatterplot exists to measure movement and dispersion away from the mean, scatter plot graphs of individual groups and subgroups can be charted to see where and what characteristics overlap. Typically, a regression model focuses on one or a few factors to solely find outliers within the measured and isolated population. When we estimate regression from relatively placed subgroups, we want to look into the exact measurements and form a regression within inversion. The mean average of each subgroup, as well as both subgroups together, is shown and weighted. Still, the truth in invertibility and cohesiveness compares regression from the mean, group to group, group to mean, and mean to a group. Comparing the mean and finding outliers is simple. Finding regression metrics with multiple population parameters in place is much more difficult, but that is where the truth will be found.

Imagine a scatter plot diagram with red points for subset one and blue points for subset two. Each issue has at least 9 points of relative measurement as opposed to only 3. When we plot the mean average regression, we look at the individual's relationship to the group from the mean, equilibrium, and other outliers. Adding each subgroup to this measurement adds a factor of 3 to each. This process will be used and depicted in the following chapters as we look as deep as possible into the relationship between global entities.

Desirable Mean Equilibrium

Mentioned in *Volume 2* is a zero point of measurement that allows for simplicity in comparison. To find a desirable mean equilibrium, we have to set this zero point. It is a difficult thing to do. It is easy to find an equilibrium point within a monetary system because data is readily available. It is much more complicated in this case because we measure dollar to dollar and dollar to ideology and thought and then belief to belief with truth and logic in the middle. It is possible, and you will see very soon how and why. The desirable mean equilibrium as a zero point then adds polarity to our diagrams and measurements. If our central point is zero, then each side, like our WVI, is set with polar opposite charges of positive and negative.

We must plot from right to left and up and down the levels of truth and outreaching extremes through a spectrum of understanding. Measurements to be applied can be very simple. At what point does a group encourage the growth and expansion of life, and does a group promote contraction and decay of life? From there, our desirable mean equilibrium begins to hold its effect. In this volume, our equilibrium is only a measurement relative to how far or close we are from our goal and at what rate the world gravitates to or away from this point. Because we are only looking through the contextual lens to understand the state of affairs, we are not quite introducing the manipulation of our model. In the previous volumes, we used equilibrium, as well as other calculations, as a constraint. In this volume, we are only looking, not melting and molding.

The Sequence of Involvement

When we begin to look at the relationships between and among global entities, a process of analysis must be in place. This ensures our relative measurements are comparable and without malignancy in our data output based on the system we run our calculations through. First, we must establish the entire universe we are looking into and then break apart our parameter metrics into groups and subgroups until we get to the demographics of every individual who lives within this universe. For the world, in this case, that is eight billion or so individuals at one end of our lens and then a set of our universe where eight billion equals one. We usually look at the demographics of groups and subgroups by numerical data if there are x number of people with y demographic. We take this exact measurement a step further and add z and then the rest of the alphabet. We look at a group and think x and y, and then why z? What involvement do sets and subsets have with one another, and why? If friction is present, we then measure the meta of ideology intertwined with demographic characteristics. It does not simply mean if one subset is purple and one subset is red; the apparent difference is hue in? No.

Our analysis does not look only at what we assume at one point in time but the progression or regression as time is constantly moving. In relativity, a purple hue from the lens of a red hued perspective is only a measure of separation not who is right or wrong. Through world events of conflict and resolution, our blue, purple and red subsets trend and accelerate toward one direction and then change course where a generic belief is irresponsible to assume. If we think of slavery in the United States, it would be foolish to think African Americans are treated worse now than during the civil war. It would also be foolish to assume, from a demographic standpoint, that all other majority races still wish slavery was present. You could say our measurement of acceleration toward progression during the civil war could hypothetically be more expansive in the right direction, than now. Some people evolve based on progress toward truth, where stagnation in belief only offers regression from our goal of unity. It is straightforward to say that African Americans were slaves to white plantation owners. That is a true statement. Even with a sensitive topic, neither side can remain stagnant with a belief system present in 1860 when the year is 2021. We cannot look at ourselves as owned by anyone, nor can we look at anyone and think we own them. We cannot look at ourselves as anything but independent from another and cannot act as a dependent on another. For cohesiveness to exist between parties to find common ground and enjoy the benefits of cooperation, we must evolve as the clock ticks irreverently.

The Zip File

If our goal is to add z values and other measurable calculations between sets and subsets, we must define our characteristics and apply complex data. Again, the difficulty is to use the rigidity a number holds to the fluidity of life and social experiences. However, in the encapsulation of our hourglass, relativity is the only way as it assumes measurement through a fluid dynamic spectrum affects all variables through the vector, changed with the ticking of time. If we are to encase our open system, it is to mark percentiles and strength in change as events occur that affect our universe. For this, we have our $AB\ i$ and B $ln\ e$, and its measurement of cohesiveness as we create a zip file.

When DNA sequencing occurs, nucleotides pair and zip up a double helix structure and replicate its process as new chemical activity is processed through time. As this ladder or zip file is built, pairs are balanced or become unbalanced where the sequence could break apart, known as chain-termination. What we do see in this process is again very similar to the relationship and involvement between celestial bodies that would hypothetically contain constantly changing mass and composition. It is hard to imagine because the sun remains the same, and so is the moon and all the stars even as mass amounts of hydrogen and helium burn. We only feel the warmth of the day. When we experience life, we do not see the collision and explosive supernovas that restructure and re-compound celestial bodies. If you were to visualize the entire universe from start to finish in one moment, you would. But, think in the gravitational terms of celestial bodies if time were ticking milliseconds but at the speed of light and apply this to the zip and unzipping of DNA structures. We analogize countries in this way and entities as celestial bodies or nucleotides involved by relative cohesiveness.

Meta Characteristics in Computation: Universal Source Code

The way we look at the world is unique to our interpretation and life experiences. Every individual sees the world differently and through a separate lens as one of 8 billion. The way we interpret clusters of individuals, however, must be through one universal looking glass. As we mentioned above, characteristics have to be compared identically from both sides and through a spectrum of color. How sequencing occurs is a process of attraction or repellant like any other alluring magnetic or gravitational system. Still, the difference is instead simple either plus or minus. We have many bonds formed by matching chemical components between simplistic polarity in attraction or repellent.

DNA nucleotides form a cohesive helix structure based on the matching of nitrogen-based compounds through base pairing. The four monomers are Guanine (G) paired with Cytosine (C) and Adenine (A) paired with Thymine (T) within the backbone as rungs of a ladder. The importance here is not that we dissect all chemical bonds within our DNA strands but know that a system of matching and sequencing exists in our world outside our physical cellular programming. Within the meta, as we measure the strength and cohesiveness between or among groups, this pairing process is analogous to how events measure the rate at which entities in the world create friction or create cohesion.

Just as sequencing DNA occurs, so do historical events that determine if a war is won, lost, or even fought at all. A very measurable cascading of principles and ideals can predict the likelihood of armed conflict or peace as the scrambling to relink strands can act in measure to prevent conflict between. Just as a chemical compound can invade a string of pairing monomers that begins to unzip our helix structure, so can an outside force positively influence the relationship between countries at odds.

For example, say the United States and Saudi Arabia are working toward the common goal of securing peace in the Middle East and decide to look past acts of lower priority of injustices against either of their people. In this isolated example, the only measurement of our ladder and zipping of our file is the partnered success toward controlling the oil fields near the Persian Gulf. An outside force or agent, or chemical compound that affects the cohesiveness is anything that prevents the desired end goal. What we look past can still bite us or poison the relationship between us. Say the end result can be affected by a relatively smaller reaction within our chain sequence. Ideologically, the United States exercises individual freedoms and rights to report prejudices through press releases. Saudi Arabia decapitates journalists. And so, the killing of an American journalist by the hands of the Saudi authorities can unzip the cohesiveness toward the end and desirable goal by no other fault but ideology. One A is paired with one C, and cohesion is rejected. The very measurable strands that exist from inception only require one strong rejection equal to all the previous pairs that have been formed.

The effort for uniformity is to place polarity against our matching compounds. For the Saudi example above, we have a malignant monomer that infiltrates the structure's ability to replicate itself and add strength to its bonds. To place uniformity in polarity as time ticks between each entity being measured, let's use a very simple example and illustrate our experiment. Let us look at a touchy subject and two people with the trade between love and money. In this exchange, we have desirability and the ability to give what is desired. We also have the strength between bonds within our source code sequencing. Remember, we are who we are because of the life experiences we have. We love based on the love we have been shown if we are not aware enough to clean ourselves from our negatively charged experiences.

Example:

Guy meets Girl at a bar. Guy or Girl has money, and Girl or Guy has desirable physical traits. Don't be triggered. It happens every damn day. What can a Guy with money give a beautiful woman with desirability? Safety, security, and comfortability. The interaction between the two begins where the glint of a gold watch sparks interest and curiosity but not the sparkle of an eye. A sequence begins, and weak bases are paired. Time continues as needs are met, but weak bonds are being paired and slowly break and unzip from the bottom upward as new weak pairs are formed, almost chasing and catching the sequencing process. As one pair is added, another below is broken. As one pair is added, three are then broken below. At one point in time, a family member of the desired needs to pay for an expensive medical procedure to which the wealthy partner decides to pay for it not out of love but out of necessity. That is enslavement with a smile. This one larger act helps speed up the pairing of bases, but more below are breaking at the same rate. What would occur if the partner decided not to pay for the medical procedure simply because it would financially ruin him or her or both of them? Time would tick, and bonds would break. Because the bonds are weak, other nitrogen-based structures would be sought out as this source code begins to fall apart and disappear. In this exchange, we have measures of strength, product input to output, and respective perception. Let's categorize these terms below for visualization:

Product Input = A: Money
Product Input = B: Love
Product Output = a: Money
Product Output = b: Love

Perspective x: Negative Charge
Perspective y: Positive Charge
The measure of strength: p-value distance from 0.

Let us name our partners in this scenario, G and Q.

G's desire = A transformed to b
Q's desire = B transformed to a

G's Inverted Cause: A = B
Q's Inverted Cause: B = A

G's Perceptual Effect (+) : a = A
Q's Perceptual Effect (-) : B = b

In terms of the above conceptual breakdown, let's look back at our example and interpret what we see in the relationship between the two people that met at a bar. First, let's think about the relationship's "birth." Just as a baby is born, so is the relationship between everyone, from friends to romantics to foes.

Every personal experience builds who they are. Still, at the point of inception of a relationship between two people, nature is the only factor, just as a baby has not been nurtured until conception or birth; However, you want to look at it. In relative terms, nurture and its effect close to the present relationship do not exist until gravity weighs its involvement measurement. Just as you walk by strangers every day, a reaction takes place. A small matched and bond pairs and then disappears without accelerated response between both parties. The genetic code, at this point, is solely the determinant trait and dominant trait because involvement has not offered a nurturing polar charged accelerant. However, in this case, everything that created the two separate individuals that walked into the bar, from both nature and nurture, acts solely as the natural genetic coding of our A and B universes.

As we zip our bonds together with each word or drink and each smile or glint of a watch or tab being paid by one or the other, chemical reactions link, cement, or break the strength of invertibility and involvement. We look at this process with polar opposite charges of separate entities or celestial masses from our process introduced in *Volume 2*. One universe is stagnated in a vast space vector while the other enters their space just enough for gravity to manipulate reality. The comparative measurement from the polar opposite spectrum is then measured as well. We explained in *Volume 2* how our A universe enters the stagnate space of our B universe and manipulates its construct and genetic makeup. What we mean then is, in relative terms, we apply this process inversely where A becomes our B to measure the juxtaposition of our space intruding universe. Why we do this is to see the involvement from both respective perspectives. If we see a positive for every negative charge or see a match within our margin of error, our sequencing can continue. If our measurement is outside the margin of error, our replication algorithm and sequencing process disappear based on first impression data.

Looking toward the genetic source code of each individual is essential to finding a matched pair of perfect invertibility and involvement. However, we must remember perfection is only a journey and acceleration toward the truth and nothing else. To find perfection is to fail because infinity is unattainable, ultimately, but the chase's speed can increase and pair to its acceleration. Based on the law of averages and measuring positive charges to negative charges is to find the strength of bonds between the subjected pairs and how they gravitate around each other. Suppose you have a data variable for lust measured at nine. Still, the ultimate truth is estimated at 0. A couple of 9's with positive and negative charges can balance around each other but truth is not the gravitational force. Lust is. The pair are perfect matches, but they are not chasing into the truth of what they think they see. Just as a couple of countries turning around the axis of evil can arbitrarily dictate, through force, the effect upon other free human beings. Just because one cause is concurrent with the other's does not mean the strength of bondage is present, only conditioned.

Convenience is present but temporary. Truth is present but long-lasting. If you are to look into the alliances after World War II, the allies have maintained a cohesive relationship because they survived together against an invasive universe of ideologies. The relationship between the United States and Great Britain is strongly irrelevant to our declaration of independence against the King because of the choice to bond to truth and cohesion against the invasiveness of authoritarianism. Even as Russia was our Ally during World War II, they are no longer seen as such. Based on ideology and bondage by convenience. Russia needed a second front against Germany, and that was Europe and the United States. Convenience lasted only until the Paris Peace Treaties. The Cold War then soon followed, where tension was mitigated but tested by space and time.

Leaving the concepts attributed to World War II to follow in later chapters, introducing the idea is imperative in our understanding here and when we draw these lines in the sand. Just as the relationship between two people is determined, so is the relationship between sets of people and large states against each other. The importance is to note the exponential growth of positive or negative forces as mass objects increase in size. One person against another can affect both parties, but not so much relative to the entire global structure. When the relationship of two people ends in tragedy tied to the assassination of archduke Ferdinand, a country is weighed against another. In Greek mythology, when the Trojan war was fought over a love interest triangle, Greece and Sparta devolved into conflict by the actions of individuals in power in emotion absent of logic.

On a sphere measuring 26,435 miles around, the distance between points and people nowadays based on technological advancement suggests there is no corner a person or country cannot influence physically and ideologically. A negatively charged ideological virus can swim through a network and convince a group of people to endorse an infamous character that will ultimately impact citizens worldwide in both positive and or negative ways. Just in the same sentence, the same shady character can reach every corner of the world with an intercontinental ballistic missile. Not so much a Neanderthal anymore, unable to conceptualize modern technology as simple as a wheel when airplane propellers are becoming futile in respect to rocket propellants. In this sense, the point of distance and space is that involvement is forced because we have grown closer and closer to each other's borders and walls. In previous centuries Europeans did not even know native Americans existed and vice versa. Now, the native American population has been catastrophically minimized.

What then does the biological makeup of our world look like for those that are deemed to be uninvolved? Just as a vector and vacuum of open space and celestial bodies swimming the ocean's open waters.

The universe exists to us as our senses allow, but that does not change the universe's reality and wholeness. Strands of DNA float through the plasma of the human body and wait to attract and replicate based on natural processes and nurtured chemical sequencing and coded methods. Again, like hardware and software.

As we skip back to our involvement between two people who met at a bar, our senses decide and react based on reactionary and programmed processes. Loud music. The odorous smell from someone you walked by or the pleasant scent of perfume. We are inoculating cocktails and concoctions of logic numbed with emotion. The brightness and calm or suspense and thrill are set by the scene of day or night. In exchange of A for b or B for a, something present and positive loses its strength to something negatively charged. When you shrink the definition of something to fit a minimal standard, it loses its value in exchange for something that only takes away from a future deal. The truth between two people is watered down based on the conversation of love for money. The law of averages weighs the strength of love as it governs all things through a war of attrition between right and wrong and good and evil.

Chain Sequencing and Termination

As a beautiful woman walks into a bar and gentlemen sit at the counter, sequencing occurs with every sense that's triggered. A bond and then a break. A bond and then a pause. A bond and bond and then a break and a break. As a gentleman asks the woman if he can buy her a drink, a bond begins, and then the reaction of yes or no decides the next bond or break. A smirk and yes is a strong bond, and then the following chemically charged pairs align. If the gentleman asks "what will it be?" A bond and then the following teams align until a negatively charged or chemical and magnetically repulsive bond is offered.

The sequence begins to terminate, and the residual nurturing effect is logged against our genetic code. Tentative response to the next offer for a drink may be subject to interpretation based on prior knowledge. Because I explain this scenario or romanticism in biological terms, I do not walk up to a lady at the bar and offer her a nucleotide. It is essential to measure and analyze the simplest yet most complex relationship between individuals as analogous to the dualistic bond between nations and states or large groups.

There are two ways a system of chain sequencing is terminated. One is based on the bonds and their strength as they build from the beginning. Another is a negatively charged super-breaker. We discussed briefly how weak bonds build over time and begin to break apart from the bottom and work their way upward toward the continuing processing point of replication. A relationship between people or parties with a weak foundation is easily destroyed as time continues and because our memory fades based on something simply not being memorable or worth remembering. That does not mean something was worthless in our journey. That means time has buried that treasure with layers of sand, but you still do not know its worth. Or, yeah, it was crap fertilizing a field to which a short period wasted its memorability away quickly. A super-breaker has much more residually present effects because it requires a supercharged chemically induced nucleotide to wreck the entire function and all the strength that has been built up. This concept acts as an anomaly to an unexpecting party to which radioactive material is left in its wake. A long time is required to clean the residual effect.

For this, our analogy between two people that meet at a bar is pretty simple. After a few weeks, months, or years or at whatever rate, one person feels something for the other, and then the other person explains they are married and have kids. It depends on the base and foundation in reality and the positivity or negativity of the un-expecting person, which would destroy the function. Even if the relationship continues, the residual effect occurs either inward or outward depending on the reciprocated polarity involved. Suppose the un-expecting party continued and pushed to remain in bondage. In that case, the other person's wife and kids experience the residual more and more dependent on at what point in time and the schematics behind the level and strength of their separately involved function that has indeed replicated over a long period.

During the event of a super-breaker, it is vital to look at the genetic compound of each entity as it is and as it has changed and is changing, and what motivation is present. A person solely founded in love would immediately leave without need or dependency unless the goal between bonded parties is above anything else. We mentioned the relationship between Saudi Arabia and the United States and a journalists' execution. The plan between entities is more important than one person's life or the residual prejudices felt by many people and citizens within respective countries.

Even as residually charged material is shot into the function, the effect is on those that they govern. It should potentially be used to weigh and sanction change for the common goal between parties not to be wasted because of the plan between parties. The point of termination is the point to which involvement ceases or inverts where friends become foes. An example of this in literature is Shakespeare's depiction of Julius

Caesar's assassination. Because ideologies began to separate leaders and parties, the effect became murder. The residual fallout caused civil war until de-escalation, and Caesar's nephew re-established a replicating function between the senate and the Emperor.

Nucleotide Comparative Definitions: Complexity of Dependent Structures

Base pairing of nucleotides happens as described in numerous textbooks on biology through the chemical compounds listed above. In our case, here, we want to illustrate what this looks like as we compare the relative position of polar opposite charges between matching helix structures as rungs of the ladder are formed. If we look at a physical strand of DNA, we notice it curves and spirals as bonds are formed. We also again know chemical bonding is rejected when an aligned chemical is not paired correctly. We add in our analogy the strength of cohesion and ability for weak or strong bonds to be formed or broken apart from bottom to top. A DNA strand that fails to replicate is unzipped based on the transmission from the present into the future, not the past to the present. We must apply this principle for a socially structured double helix even if it is not biologically sound. It, however, will make sense as we apply polarity and strength between structures along a solid goal founded in truth and goodwill. Let's have a look:

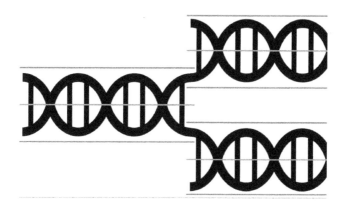

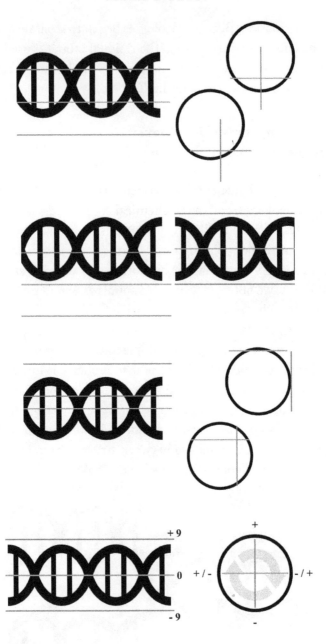

Within the above figures, we see the depiction of different process types and functions of DNA pairing. Analogy aside, let's look at the actual biological process that occurs when DNA is zipped and "unzipped," as discussed above.

Process Type: Measurement in Cohesion and Involvement

Transcription

We describe the process better known as gene expression, where DNA segments function based on conditions within each cell. The term Transcription is defined as the process of copying a part of DNA into RNA using enzymes. The enzyme binds to a segment of DNA and breaks apart hydrogen bonds connecting cohesive DNA nucleotides. Transcription acts to form different types of RNA known as tRNA, mRNA, and rRNA as derivatives of the initial DNA.

Translation

The process to which genetic coding is read within cellular biology is known as the translation process. Translation takes place in steps where start codon acts to initiate the deciphering of gene code, elongation where interaction between ribosomes, amino acids, and tRNA create an amino acid chain, and then termination when the process of translation is terminated known as stop codon. This process involves tRNA transports amino acids to the ribosome to create a polypeptide.

Replication

When two identical strands of DNA are created from one, the biological process is known as replication. A helicase separates the helix structure allowing for free-floating nucleotides to pair and create a new double helix structure. It results in chromosomes formed as partial or complete units of genetic code dependent on the mitotic phase state.

Key terms in the transcription, translation, and replication processes that occur in a cell we should note and apply a parallel analogy to are as follows: cell body, nucleus, DNA, RNA, nucleotides, ribosomes, polypeptide, protein synthesis, start and stop codon, amino acid chain, single and double stands, helices, polymerase, ligase, and replication fork. Defined and Applied as:

Cell Body: A large subset within the universe.

Cytoplasm: Universe vector of space allowing and sustaining life and component interaction.

Nucleus: The population within the subset subject to involvement and effectible upon the cell body.

DNA: Genetic source code of isolated or involved pairs.

RNA: Event carrier in different forms holding a polar charge for manipulation. Residual and inverted polarity code from the pairing process.

Nucleotides: Sensory polarity charge between individuals carrying genetic code from relative perceptible positions and reciprocity in an inversive state when pairing.

Base Pairing: True or False cohesive principle.

Ribosomes: Catalyzation of an event and interpretation setting.

Polypeptide: Tool creating potential cause and effect from event catalyzation.

Protein Synthesis: Effective event process of new information.

Start and Stop Codon: Trigger of involvement and cohesion or termination of algorithm function.

Amino Acid Chain: Predictable action upon an event and the effect that follows. Characteristics and demographics of the individual or measured population that crosses the event horizon energy threshold.

Single and Double Strands: Isolated or involved pairs.

Helicase: Divergent event.

Polymerase: Chance or destined event bringing code carriers within sensory proximity.

Ligase: Readjustment and compromise to relink and reset the pairing process from misfired or misinterpreted relationship.

Replication Fork: Unzipping site of old bonds to be replaced by new compatible code.

With the above terms in place, we can step into the process and interpretation on a socio-biological level. The process of DNA replication and other functions of genetic coding at the micro-level is imperative to our understanding of the macro level. Just as our system is open, our goal is not to close it but encapsulate it to understand every moving part. What we see in the chemical properties and movement of microscopic particles is that life itself is complex. Still, it follows very rigid rules invariant from the process but subject to the openness of the environment. As chemical compounds are added, others are moved or subtracted. Sure, a simple interpretation but a true one. Varying levels of essentiality are placed where some are more utilized than others. Still, a cell dies when one small particle fails, or killed by a disease or virus that is introduced, slowly weakening the host's body. We may stray a bit from the popular understanding of DNA replication and biological processes in the following chapters but in a hypothetical scientific method. We are not here to say anything arbitrarily. However, we are here to ask the question, "What gives our way of living the life it has?"

Our continued effort along the biological level in this volume is just that question and not yet offers the absoluteness a solution has. In mathematical terms, a solution is an end-all and rigid definition of what is what. With the complexity of our study, we have not looked deep enough to find that quite yet. So the purpose of this volume remains to look through the lens of history with new information, hopeful, to cut a picture clear and persistent enough to know with absolute certainty, at some point, what the future could and would hold. As we continue down into the center of the earth, let us think of our effort as investigators and detectives and not judge and jury. We are not to the trial phase, but we must know true and falsehood should be expected without acquittal.

Perfection, however, in absolute certainty is trivial and only found in a system closed to perceptible growth. An open mind will see a model in the velocity to which the chase into the sun continues unending. Just as lust acts inversely to the truth of how we love someone, love breaks all rigidity of form while lust binds to rigidity in mistruth. Perfection in an open system is not attainable as a place to be reached but a dimension to be pushed and expanded. Where perfection by design is unattainable, its measurement, as a goal, is a variable's increasing velocity relative to the rate of system expansion. In a closed system, perfection is attainable, but that is not one we inhabit. Where evil retracts variable potential relative to the walls of a secure system, good expands the system itself and takes all other variables with it. And now, let's look into this lens of history and analyze how Mr. and Mrs. Caveman became so rude.

Tracking Growth and Decay Through Historical Global Affairs

The succeeding text is what I have looked forward to writing the most since finishing volume one. Without the bulk of interpreted material penned, papered, and stored, further adaptations and analysis would be impossible. Just the same as we look into the past, this volume could not exist either without penning the first, nor could the future of our potential be reasoned without what happens now.

Civilization was not born from anything at one singular moment in time but grew from present energy potential optimized without waste, for the most part. Whether good or bad, growth or decay, positive or negative, everything in history has brought humanity to the moment we live in now. We have pandemics, but we have medical achievements. We have wars but extended periods of peace. We have tension but also healing. We have stupidity, but also scholars. We have economic retraction but periods of growth. We have totalitarianism but also freedom, so we think. We have communism but also democracy and capitalism. We don't have anything we do not create from within. What we do have, we utilize for the benefit of some and the expense of another. The sociological status today is because of all of our yesterdays, whether dark or bright.

Looking back in time, we do an injustice to our study in picking one point of reference because that is not the truth of the matter. However, I was not present when the universe was formed but I can imagine it. Just as our journey into perfection is just a journey, we can measure and build our understanding not based on being present when a system was created but by analyzing our own story in relative terms. With a good memory and ability to throw new principles into the melting pot of interpretation against historical events, an understanding can solidify a cast like a metal molding holding our foundation of reason. The journey of humanity and our involvement with one another start in the tribes of hunters and gatherers that fought other savages over food and minor resources. Going back and forth in time, Egyptian emperors built pyramids and aqueducts on the backs of a group I never met nor was present to determine their lineage as Israelites or any other culture or creed.

We are not here to argue the validity of historical events that are not well documented but set the stage. Roman leaders went to war against all factions of early Europe to expand their domain. Crusades swept early lands and left nothing but bloodshed. Greece, Sparta, and the Persian armies still live mythologically, read by students in school, only because recorded history becomes murky and mythological the further we look back. Genghis Khan led Mongolians into other territories for dominance in Asia, all while Native Americans were clueless to the rest of the world. Clash between Spaniards and the Aztecs soon changed the genetic makeup of the indigenous population inhabiting the Americas. Mayans and Amazonian tribes, still isolated today, created math and scientific principles in studying the stars also used still to this day. Vikings and other barbarians of the North Atlantic and Arctic Sea influenced both Northern Europe and American continents. Napoleon lived longer in infamy than he did in living his short life.

Enough of war, but what about inventions? We mentioned the study of the stars in South America but also great inventors and influencers in Europe. Socrates, Plato, Aristotle, Copernicus, Galileo, Bacon, Descartes, Newton, etc. We study structures that predate even 15th-century explorers and thinkers. The Romans with archways, aqueducts, and concrete structures. The pyramids and city systems in Egypt and South America. Stonehenge. The Great Wall. Pulley systems. Tools used by cultivators or artisans. Early tribes used clay pots and pans. Caves turned to huts, cabins, homes, and then large marble structures and marvels such as the coliseum or temples throughout China, India, or the Middle East. Weaponry from sticks and stones to iron and steel swords and arrows with chainmail or armored plates and helmets. Sandals and moccasins and then boots replaced the pain of being barefoot. The embarrassment of bare-nakedness only became a thing once we used bearskin to keep warm from the elements and then cotton to spin shirts, blouses, and pants.

Culminating the start of our analysis, we look to the Renaissance and the intellectual, scientific revolution. Why here? Because this is where cognition is a rocket engine ignited and soon to follow is the modernization of the world we see first-person every day. Let it be noted, the only two accelerants are resources and ideology.

The Scientific Revolution: 17th Century

The importance of the Scientific Revolution and Renaissance is relevant to all matters and aspects of life today. The way the world is viewed now owes a debt of gratitude to thinkers of the Renaissance. Rational thought replaced belief as we began to study the world God created for what it was and not only what it symbolized. Gravitation away from orthodox faith made room for an empirical thought process through observation absent of blindly following what someone says. The pen-paper of writing this book correlates directly with the introduction of the scientific method 350 years prior. As a defining period in time, wonder began to pry the hands of arbitration from reality's throat for us to breathe pure oxygen but we still gasp for more.

Cause

To look at the reason for any historical event, through an empirical formula of observation, we must look at the cause. Societal growth in involvement demands both governing and governed bodies to ask and require new ways of life. It is easy to suffocate an idea watered down by the request of one individual. It is much more complicated when adverse side effects are undeniable and unavoidable. No longer could we deal with the starvation of thousands of people who are to go without food. Feeding one family is a simple task. Feeding cities full to the brim is another. The demand for mass production and simplification of processes could not rely solely on belief. One person can survive, for some time, on raindrops falling from the heavens to fill a jug. What is required to sustain the way of life of large populations is one complexity to match another complexity as another arises. An aqueduct collects rainwater the same way, but the necessity to route an essential resource is essential. The old belief that it will surely rain cannot accommodate millions of people in Los Angeles. A new way of thought in the abstract to build dams and reservoirs and predictive measures that determine if tropical oceanic weather patterns will bring rain or drought is required and the science is complex. The universe has a funny way of showing you exactly what you need when you need it, almost to answer a request before you give it as if a stranded neanderthal is thinking about how to build a raft to reach the mainland.

Abstract thought led to analytical reasoning—the scientific process of confirming or denying the absurd allowed for absurdity to validate itself. As a caveman observes and tastes a carcass cooked by a wildfire, he knows cooking meat makes it taste good. Progression is always met with resistance regardless of the apparent validity of thought and reason behind a study. Usually, research and solutions are founded by many more calculated hours than its judgment even allows. As the leader of the Scientific Revolution, Galileo is both the physical and spiritual symbol of this process. Not only imprisoned but blasphemed for a thought that turned out to be correct. It occurs today and even at this moment. Nothing so absurd as heliocentrism can be pondered by someone unwilling to look through a telescope. The irony of the charge of heresy is it's the simple definition of questioning authority. If you ask a question big enough, it will question all authority where irony rests in this question's answer that brings you closer to the God a heretic is punished over. In due time, though not having enjoyed the fruits of his findings, the truth is apparent and widely accepted, but with a stain. Like a white shirt in a washing machine discolored by a red sock, the fault is not his own, but the consequences and effect are at this moment.

Conflict: Orthodox Belief vs. the Scientific Method

The result? The world you have today is absent of complete barbarism. The world would likely not exist without intellectual growth at this necessary and pivotal transformation period required for sustaining life. Imagine Newton murdered for heresy and documents set ablaze, or Galileo hung or beheaded in the street for questioning an unarguable but false, absolute truth. Imagine the entirety of civilization demeaning, discrediting, and disagreeing with the answer that proves all other truths that are unable and un-allowed to be questioned as fallacious, hollow and nothing further from the truth.

A doctor would not have formed the correct mixture of components to cure a common cold, let alone treat an infectious disease. Air travel would still be sinful. Through a system of transformation of input to output, the effect is always a strenuous process of molting, melting, bending, and breaking input variables and reorganizing genetic coding. Still, the output is always stronger than what entered. Just as looking out to the stars allowed us to look toward the atom, nuclear warheads exist but also the deterrent against their use. Just as steel is formed from heat and pressure, the mixture of iron and carbon through a furnace, so are our leaders of the continued Scientific Revolution. Further below, we take inventory of the changes made during our 17th-century tuning into reality and isolating cohesion and friction along category lines inscribed by historical events.

Ideology and Belief Systems

Greek ideology persisted to influence everyday life into the early 17th century. Belief dominated bewilderment and wonder. Process denial dominated a process of reason. The attempt to implement a scientific method was successful but heavily pushed back against. At this moment in history, the heaviest fight for progression was met with the most severe resistance. Still, progression broke free regardless of the number of free thought provokers imprisoned by negligent logic and reasoning. Egyptian slaves likely thought of freedom but were zombified by and subdued by whips and aggression. Space, or the illusion of its allowance in thought, prevented violent overthrow during the Renaissance. The right to free speech is a right in modern-day because every subdued voice subdues truth. The world would be a different place if geocentrism were the truth we lived by or if heliocentrism was a truth discredited. Subjected conflict in ideology during the 17th century are as followed:

The threat of Influence: Authoritative Source of Information About Heaven and Earth

The threat in itself to population influence was met naturally by a pushback by the Roman Catholic church when astronomers looked into the heavens. The Greek ideology of planetary movement subject to the control of the Gods was met with apprehension when calculative measures put quantitative values against reasoning. As opposed to Zeus reigning supreme, gravity did. A monolithic approach was present in the Catholic church that replaced many gods with one god, but the same question was applied not to question God but to question how God programmed the universe's movement. Not so much, again, the existence of an entity, whether believed or not, but the entity's fingerprint on the universe in its creation. To look into the heavens was to see very minute crevasses in a thumbprint when all we understood was the hand.

Location Conflict: Roman Catholic Church's Center

Friction is naturally created between two parties at odds with proximal locality as a factor. The Roman Catholic Church might have annihilated the Aztecs and Mayans or even the Egyptians if they lived next door. However, throughout Europe, the Renaissance posed a pinpointed threat against the church solely by space in time. It is argued ideals of the Renaissance did not come about exclusively in Europe and solely in this period, but the culmination of ideologies into one uniform scientific method is apparent based on Galileo's imprisonment or Bruno's burning at stake; both for heresy. In truth or not, when an opposing party questions an authoritarian principle, the apparent effect is shown in cases like Galileo and Bruno. Even as Copernicus was friendly with the Orthodox Catholic Church, the Protestant Sect of Christianity had significant issues with his thoughts of the heavens.

If the Renaissance were not a culmination taking place in this time and space, tensions would likely have resulted in weaker acts against those that spoke out. Like a pot of boiling water, heat causes molecules to expand and evaporation to take place. If the boiling point were higher or if less heat were added, perhaps the result would not be what it is documented as. I highly doubt the Roman Catholic Church's ability to burn someone at the stake if they lived in Asia minor. But, yes, scientists throughout the continent of Asia were also persecuted for belief against authority, whether in god or country.

The Cohesion of Science and Religion in Art

Copernicus's involvement with the Catholic Church is evident that the two can coexist. If you cozy up to an authoritarian, it at least delays the inevitability of persecution. I would even go as far as to say Copernicus's involvement with the Catholic Church delayed the Renaissance from taking place earlier. The search for a gray area between black and white is easier in relieving tension than when one argues boldly against the other regardless of who is right or wrong. In reality and the search for absolute truth, both will always remain wrong because the truth is something never fully grasped or felt, just as a singularity is an infinitely dense space in time.

The use of artwork worked to find that gray area without submitting to tense and rigid guidelines. Anatomical drawings of the science of the human body and paintings of the heavens began to link science and the church in a way words never could. Michelangelo & Da Vinci, among others, show this in their inventions and creations. One can admire the act of god while also explaining the scientific reasoning behind design and us as a creation. In a somewhat hidden motivation and sneaky way, the point was made. Perhaps this is why movies and books written about scientific revolutionaries in the arts are so much fun to watch or create because the motive is never a truth firmly defined.

Galileo: Round vs. Flat Earth 1633

Contrary to some not so popular opinions, the Earth was determined to be round by Galileo's calculations and observation in 1633. Using his invention of the telescope, which opened the door to thousands of other possibilities, Galileo physically confirmed calculations to determine this without fighting internet warriors against the simple study and fact. It is easy to fool someone unwillingly to look through a lens they did not create. Where a telescope is symbolic of the physical, it is also a symbol of logic and reasoning. You cannot force an opinion in a free-thinking world. The two thoughts fight each other. You can offer further understanding even if their denial leaves a residual effect upon you and the rest of the world. It continues today and is depicted symbolically during the Renaissance of natural conflict against progression irrelevant of fact and further truth and understanding.

It is hard to nicely tell someone they are wrong because emotion captivates reasoning where logic is their prisoner. The Church maintained geocentrism as well as the flatness of the Earth as a creation of God. Stating the Earth is round does not disprove the latter; however, it questions the motive of saying why the Earth would be flat because, at this point, rationalization against is a misconstrued interpretation as a rebuttal that God must not have created it. That is faulty reasoning in itself. The Earth can be round and created by God, but faith is the determinant of creation to which no scientist in history has proven to be true or false. It, quite frankly, will remain as such, and we will be better for interpreting the universe instead of deciding ourselves without reason, something that is calculated by non-physical phenomena to which calculations are unquantifiable. Any investigation into the sciences proves only existence as to how but not why, who, or what.

Governance and Commerce: Humanism

Humanism adopted a spreading belief that morality should govern a social society as a set of laws of the natural world. Natural law, in astronomy, biology, chemistry, and anatomy was emerging with the implications of the empirical process. Again, a massive concern of the church as the authority figure. The population requested humanism to subject interaction within a social structure based on generically assumed morals and social norms. They typically expressed atheist and agnostic beliefs. They were acting as a substitute to the Roman Church's authority, humanists aligned with no god simply working as the inverse of the church's position. Complete unquestioned alignment with the fear of God required a substitute and inverted fight at the front lines.

A point by humanists could not be made if the basic alignment did not venture far enough away from traditional norms. As a product of the universe itself, this was the effect. Because Roman Catholicism established authority based on the principle of divinity, the army against complete control assembled around the ideology hedged that humanity should replace divinity. This thought is insidiously present even more nowadays where individuals act for themselves but shade motivation behind the divinity of God where their actions align with the deity of self. Humanists did not believe divinity was in man nor god, but morality could replace the construct of authority and keep others and the government responsible for their actions. It became misconstrued with an evolution along the mass production of faulty logic. When humanists say we should remove God's divinity at the forefront, they stated morality of man should govern. They did not say the divinity of man.

The Ideal Citizen

Machiavelli wrote of the virtue of the human soul to always strive to be virtuous when dealing in affairs with others. Perhaps not a definition solely written from Machiavelli but a derivative from his process of thought. Laws of man should be enforced based on the strive for virtue within ourselves and within others. Hope is created that this search is complementary and not compromising, as was God's divinity as an enforcer through incomplete interpretation of man in ruling one another. Realism, as the rejection of assumption and adherence to observation, as a process of interaction grew as a dominant social science. The belief that human dignity could compute a variable through collective reason allowed humanity to apply natural law.

If an ideal citizen were to exist, the definition of virtue was congruent with willingness and want to become educated. It was not enough to own a book but to understand and then further pick apart the context to enable self-analytical, interpretation, and actualization. It was not enough for a citizen to accept the truth without adding context. A silent response is worth nothing in the view of realism. In reality, the humanist approach contextualizes and applies to each individual an openness of the system within. Enlightenment to a humanist is the same process as the universe's creation. It is not to close our method of understanding because natural law suggests otherwise. As the term Renaissance equates to rebirth or awakening, this era is the human mind's ability to open a once closed system, itself. Like cracking an egg, the light only gets in if it's rattled and stressed and forced to for survival.

Child Growth in Society

As literary principles grew in essentiality, books and libraries became important and intriguing forms to self-educate and socialize. Studies from all over Europe and Asia were centralized in large buildings to be learned from. No longer was owning a book an odd thing. Instead, holding a book was a sought-after and desirable luxury because knowledge attainment was social status attainment. Just as a question used to be met by brute force, society was founded on brute strength and physical labor.

A question was being asked, as input systems of understanding and encouragement were now requiring new advancements to keep up with a new social system and other industries. Instead of trading three goats for one mule, we began to exchange knowledge and information and a combination of the previous and latter. Nowadays, we finance large farms where documentation and monetary systems are traded to feed many citizens. This is the direct result of education as a standardized norm and not a simple and odd benefit not required in previous history. The shame is an unwillingness to learn as opposed to an interest to learn.

When a child might ask a parent in the 14th century, "what is that shiny thing in the sky at night?" The parent may have replied with, "that's the dark time light god gave us." Now, we simply say, "that's the moon and phases as its position relative to the sun offering more light on some nights and less on others." Just as a child left with a group of apes in the jungle, Tarzan grew up not understanding where ships came from when they pulled ashore. The importance of child growth was imperative because intellectual growth in society became imperative to society and the individual.

Social Morality and Individual Virtue: Democracy and Rationality

The freedoms in the United States today are directly correlated to enlightenment principles of the Scientific Revolution. Freedom of speech, thought, and expression exists because Galileo sat in prison and lived the rest of his life a prisoner in his own home. Whether Galileo was right or wrong is irrelevant from our perspective. Only partially correct in the grander scheme, he was right enough at the time to instill the belief that an authority legitimized by force is not legitimate at all. Social morality and individual human virtue is the direct cause of democracy as the positive to authoritarianism's negative charge. Just as humanism creates a system of complementary principles and values, it removes only compromise. Sure, compromise is appropriate in diplomacy but not the requirement around truth in a discussion. I would even say humanism's use of the word compromise as the definitive principle of authoritarianism is nice of them but probably not correct. Arbitrary or arbitrariness is probably more correct. Just as three separate but equal branches act in complementary ways, laws within the Constitution are written to prevent anything else. If the system does not complement the people, then it is incorrect in its application. But, like any growing science or ideological principle, at what point does the population of governed citizens outgrow these laws and compromise in general application? The answer is at the same rate to which the Scientific Revolution became necessary and a necessity to facilitate the continuity of momentous growth where the laws of nature as they are discovered will always require updating the laws that govern people. As committed as we are required to be, the resolution must continue its evolution to replace an investigation and resentment among those that question as cohesive principles must outlast adhesive properties. As the shallowness of a thin layer of water attached to the surface dries into nothingness, the ocean's depth loses nothing in relative terms to the whole. But, alignment to reason fades with each loss in exchange.

New Thinking and New Technology; Commerce Required

Think, if the openness of thought was wilder in the 17th century than it was, and Galileo observes the moon is solid gold with his telescope. At his point, imagine the only obsession was then to reach the moon and an entire civilization just as obsessed. Natural growth landed humanity on the moon in 1769 instead of 1969. This is quite impossible without the industrial revolution taking place, but a purpose and drive require alternative measures and ways of life. As new inventions were created, new avenues were also required just the same. By creating large libraries with important texts, a system of checking books out is created. As humanism emerges, taxation and law and order have to be placed in resolve when someone cannot pay their debts. Paying Michelangelo to paint the Sistine Chapel requires a payment system and one to ensure the paint he uses is adequate. Trading cows and chickens for the Mona Lisa just doesn't work the same. Where taxation for protection by giving sheep or wives to a king was required, or you'd be shamed or killed became outdated, a system of social sustenance replaced physical protection with the protection of a pursuit for intellect and social investment. Sure, the 17th century was absent of many relatively valued luxuries that we have today, like a shower, but the Dark Ages were called the Dark Ages for a reason.

Intellectual property and power became a value above physical ability. As the demand for new knowledge became idealized, its value followed. New inventions and improvements of systems of production were the delayed result of the Renaissance. Observing how an engine could be utilized with an axle and wheels or turn a prop through trial and error was only the benefit of humanity years later. The importance of the scientific revolution related to commerce is not an effect directly seen during the period but in the years to follow and hinted previously as an introduction into the Industrial Revolution discussed in the following chapters.

Into the Future: A Lingering Effect

Looking through the looking glass at history in isolating the 17th century as a pivotal point for humanity has its deeper reasoning against this book than you may think. Before we jump into historical events, we looked at something very different as the cellular biology of relationships between individuals or entities. Our purpose is not to leave that thought in the dust as we leap into hyperspace but be our warp drive machine propelling us through space. The scientific revolution placed intellectual effect upon an unconscious population. The complexity of society before the turn measured success by survival instead of a population's ability and capability to thrive. In our biological model, involvement between entities is very simply put. If we isolate the conflict between polar opposite parties during this time, we have the Church and scientists. Cohesion is attempted, but adhesive principles dominate society. Even as Copernicus attempts to stay involved with the Catholic Church, nucleotide bonds of understanding continue to falter and fall apart based on the genetic makeup to accept what could be or deny what is. Imagine a double helix structure with constantly breaking base pairs attempting to reattach and social divergent helicase events or observations continually driving each amino acid chain apart. With every word uttered by a scientist, an attempt to translate and transcribe new RNA strands to rebuild the genetic building blocks of the relationship between church and state remained futile in pairing logic to truth in commonality. However, constant pressure and involvement overwhelmed the process and forced no code to be readjusted and resubmitted into replication until it became required by the masses. As populations grew and demanded change in governance the Roman Catholic Church was forced to submit to survive themselves.

The introduction of historical events placing the scientific revolution as a foundational point is not to use what happened here to test our cellular process nor invertibility and involvement calculations. Looking into the complexity of peace and war since the Renaissance is to understand the rewriting of genetically coded A and B universes happened here where thought accelerants became more potent for good as well as evil. Looking into the good and miraculous, our look into the future begins with the industrial revolution that followed and continued cascading effects of opening a closed system. For all purposes, we live in the universe, and we understand that we are subject to the laws that exist as we know them as well as some we do not. In 10,000 BC, our universe was a closed system with the sky as a dark painted wall. Today, it is as open as ever with our understanding of the universe's constant expansion into the abyss. No physical properties of the universe changed, but perception changed the natural laws we live and abide by. Most say you cannot claim to have invented physics because it was only discovered. Partially true. To a caveman living by the law of survival, you invented a new way of life, not only the study of it just as a system or the machine that turns butter or spins cotton or wool to create clothing. You can, however, create inventions based on the laws of physics that can take you to the moon. Understand the universe and her laws enough and you can reach the edge where all reason begins.

The Industrial Revolution

Rediscovery and analysis of classical philosophy, looking and questioning the stars and the heavens, lead to new processes of ingenuity. The revolution of enterprise required a new social system to encapsulate it. Ramped up production equated to ramped up population growth where urbanization replaced farmer and tenant systems. Through simple supply and demand, for every new means of production, a factory worker was required. Through the opposite side of the spectrum, for every new worker or member of the social population, production was required and depended upon for the population's survival. In the same way, higher rates of production mixed with urbanization are simultaneously causes and effects of one another. During the Dark Ages, this give-and-take and reciprocation could not be described. Why?

A closed system presided over arbitrariness in "you make, I take," said the King. As we rapidly expand the opening of a system of production, a cycle is created just as what we describe in *Volume 1*. As it rains, through space and time, a stream is filled that leads to the ocean where consumption ensures inhabitants thrive, and then evaporation recharges a constantly moving system much more complex than before. The complexity lies in the involvement of individuals against the collective. In replacing individual farmers that feed only themselves with multinational corporations and trading companies, the time it would take to sell crops to someone in East India by bringing you goats and milk is too much. Space and time, properties of physics and astronomy, created the need to replace bartering with commodity and monetary value through a new market of exchange. For growth, shares of stock were sold by multinational conglomerates just as a family farm would sell their own livestock. Complexity replaced simplicity in trade.

New Capabilities Require New Abilities and Vice Versus

Invention and ingenuity worked congruently to add innovation where innovation was required as Europe, and surrounding nations readopted a new approach to classical philosophy, problem-solving increased. The most famous invention during this time was the steam engine, as we mentioned previously. As the world began to understand the essentiality of fire and heat, we learned of its chemical and beneficial properties. We are not just a caveman bewildered by a radiant heat magically crisping a carcass but elaborately investigating the principles that would lead to power plants and electricity. The steam engine solved a problem and added a different solution. First, as it was used in the 17th century, the steam engine cleared flooded coal mines to increase production efficiency and mitigate risk. Not only are we using heat and coal to power an engine but circumventing the process of supply and demand. Think directly in the case of a steam engine pumping flooded water from a mine to extract coal and other metals. We are using the product we are mining to allow us to extract that same product.

This is how systems are made, and intellectual growth creates problems solved. We extract coal or iron ore that heads to a smelter that creates essential components and then returns to the mine, in some fashion, to assist in extracting the same material—processes of efficiency in this way act to mitigate the effects and optimize consumption. Where coal may have made its way to only the smelter and never returned to the mine, consumption, and value hold only a one sum value. Through a transformation cycle and system, we created new sum value dimensions and exponentially increased not only the system's value but value in each component as well. Time replaces space. Efficiency, as well as survival, is now dependent on this cycle continuing. Good or bad? Both.

Our reliance on technology is one not to look lightly into. It allows for increased production and new possibilities but also the possibility of catastrophe if our system fails. A universe 100% percent made up of technological code and robots is stagnant if one line of code shuts down the central server. At this point, life ends because a miracle would require a lifeless robot to repair itself. However, that is the beauty of humanity and life as a miracle in itself charged by a seemingly unending power.

As production increases, piles of coal or other ore are stocked without the necessary locomotive ability to transport raw material to be smelted. The same cyclical process as above repeats, and the steam engine evolves to power a rotational energized piston replacing a one beam valve. Now, you have a train. The revolution of commerce is present and based in the space and time of the scientific revolution in the previous century. As Galileo looked into a different space and time through a telescope, so did the rest of the world. A train is the physical product of this new approach. As Galileo questions our understanding of space and time, we question our own. In commerce, the time it takes to relocate space to space in time is just the same as new technologies are invented. The need to move large piles of coal and raw material through space is time-sensitive in our cyclical way of commerce and dependent upon implemented mechanisms. Mechanical thinking and new mechanisms, again, were a result of the Renaissance and new scientific understanding. The question, as it applies to our biological coding and *ABi* and *B ln e*, what one factor manipulates our coding enough that allows us to grow and expand into this new world of thought? Accelerant potency.

Friction Produced From an Inventory of Inventions

Acting to add potency to humanity's rocket fuel is much more than just the steam engine and telescopic lens. Cement, gas-lighting, textile mechanisms, cotton, machine and navigation tools, paper machines, glass making, revolutions in mining and agriculture, roads and railways, the factory system of production, and increased living standards were all additions. Still, they did not encompass every revolutionized ingredient in our system's recipe for growth. Even as beneficial as every invention was and is, a cost is always paid. Where urbanization around the factory system allowed for mass production, the negative implications of child labor and environmental impact were felt as production continuity of momentum is required at all cost. The mass production of commodities planted the seed for the unequal acquisition of equity. Advantageous as we are, a snowball effect always is present beyond what we see first person in time. A child doesn't understand the factory owner's position to create personal wealth. That child only understands rules, authority, and hunger. The urbanization of central Europe allowed for the centralization of global production to spur its effect felt throughout the world. Textile machinery and transportation abilities leaped lightyears ahead of countries without the same technological advancements. Nations were formed. In previous centuries borders were lines in the sand and were murky at best, moving back and forth with force and war. An intellectual brick wall now fortified the nation within against the nation without and out at their gates. Transactions made by the clashing and clanging of swords are replaced with transactions through the main gate with only the fear of force and the unknown to protect each trader involved in commerce with one another. As populations grow, the push against the dividing wall becomes troublesome and problematic for both parties, where force once a threat may become inevitable.

Navigational tools and instruments created a wonder of what is beyond and the ability to get there placed negative effects upon forms of life that were found beyond the walls of the understood world. At this point in time during the industrial revolution, colonization of the Americas is already occurring with the navigational tools they had at this point. The benefit of finding new worlds and new resources is good for the overall collective but not the subgroups that inhabit each new world. Wherever we look, relatively large groups of migrants moving into new worlds act as an invasive species bringing disease and unrecognized legitimacy to natives. Nowadays, the world is much different where law and order are usually clearly established and disease much more controllable if the migrant population is a relatively small measurement against the population of natural inhabitants. As the Spaniards and North American colonizers moved into the new world, destruction followed as friction reached a point of no return for natives. In a statistical sense, the overall mean average benefited at the expense of a subgroup of "outliers." Pillage and plunder did not discriminate as peaceful populations are forced to protect their own against modern weaponry, disease formed in a ship's hull now docked onshore, and "belief" in the divinity of man's self-declared divine attachment to and alignment with the concept of manifest destiny.

Nations formed became the staple of representation where force against a nation's people asks a question to be looked down upon. Now, yes, austere authoritarians are still more present than accepted, relatively speaking. The movement made toward an equilibrium state between citizens and authority is noted. Quite possibly, the most potent accelerant created from the industrial revolution isn't the factory system nor urbanization, nor the steam engine or gas-lighting—the paper machine. As large numbers of people are centralized in a small space in time, conversation and communication form ideas from the heart of their collective to ask a question now available to be spread like wildfire through the world. Galileo's question is asked but suppressed based on not letting a question breathe free air. Printing hundreds of thousands of the same question on a piece of paper can be sent throughout continental Europe and into Asia before an idea can be suffocated. Time beats space. Books on all the inventions listed above and more can now make their way out of libraries and into the streets, farms and villages. The new world is created not once reaching the golden gates but when the news of it can be transported on the backs of thin cuts of a tree and oil-based ink. The paper machine as a physical invention and creation of counting systems and machines exists as an alliteration of what is to come from their amalgamation; the digital machine. Hardware and software.

Progression

We know, by observation, progression is always met with conservation of the norm though conservation is not directly attributed to our genetic programming to grow. Polarity, though, is. Positivity is always balanced by negativity, but positivity seems to always edge negative charges by one degree. How? The ultimate question in our discussion is just that, how. Suppose we look through a new telescope in the 17th century or the Kepler version as an evolution of that same telescope but in modern times. The growth and evolution of ideals are always based on the accelerant involved. The 'why and what' is an accelerant against the 'how' even if we do not understand how nor fully understand why and what. Galileo's look into the stars is only a further answer to 'what.' Looking at the simplicity of how a question is phrased is a tactful approach in analyzing the question itself and questions asked through history that led to an effectible change in progressive velocity. It is then useful to look at the shape of the answer and how it was phrased as a compromise, arbitration, or in compatibility.

As rocket fuel for humanity, the accelerant affects the genetic coding involved in growth and involvement between asking and answering parties. Just as the replication, translation, or transcription of involved entities is a measurement of understanding, each separate process acts differently to manipulate our coding as an individual to the collective or vice versa. Mechanically speaking, fuel does nothing to the overall mechanical components of a system of energy output. Fuel, in its potency, does act as a result of cause and effect and is necessary to keep up with a mechanism's further evolution. A rocket engine could not carry a shuttle into the upper atmosphere if it were a product of energy created by steam. The chemical properties during a change in elemental state does not produce enough energy. As we look further into the sciences, we begin to create more complex propellants requiring more potent sources of energy. Just as a locomotive moves hundreds of tons of coal, at some point in time and space, as growth increases by an exponential variable, a new engine is required to maintain growth in homeostasis. Homeostasis is not simply remaining in one firm elemental state but, in fact, a firm elemental state securely cohesive to the exponential constant of growth.

How does positive charge always beat negativity by one degree through space in time is the same as this analogy. If we were programmed to decay, negativity would steal that degree in every transaction. Catastrophe remains the danger as the balance between becomes increasingly dynamic. Like a snowball rolling down a hill building speed and mass, at the point of contact with the side of a structure, the snowball disintegrates without residual effect or us evening noticing. As time goes on, the hill gets higher and steeper and filled with more loose snow until that snowball becomes an avalanche that wipes out an entire village. This is what we are trying to prevent even with our relentless effort, as good maintains dominance by at least a degree. Just as plant and animal species act to repopulate and survive with Darwinist tendencies, so do we as individuals, as a collective, and then as the system our collective fuels.

The irony in most things is the reciprocity we see in seeing the unseen. Just as we are our biological makeup, our biology makeup is who we are. The relationship and cohesion between two people is the relationship of polarity we have in ourselves. We are the choices we make, but we are not the choice itself rather a culmination of *who*, *what*, *where*, *when*, and *how* we are nurtured. The scientific revolution and Renaissance acted to introduce questions into all forms of life on earth when *why* the only answer was was given to divinity's rule. We are a product of our experience on earth and by the free will to decide how we act in certain situations by the parameters the universe gives us. Most people think God reigns in every aspect, and that is not completely false but also not completely true either. Suppose we are free-willed beings who encounter events throughout our own personal history that add up to the sum of all human history. In that case, God can cause us to encounter certain genetically structured scenarios but cannot create nor decide the experiences we have or form. As I sit here on pi day in the year 2021, God may have written the code of the universe based on pi and phi, but we control whether we become triangles or squares or retreat to the circular and cyclical fundamentals of the universe. By a product of God's design yes we are free to choose but not free from what we choose as our choice is another line of predetermined coding added to our genetic makeup.

Man's Divine Path Forward

As man replaces God with himself in the effort of self-realization, the path forward into the inevitable is war. The authority principle attributed to the divinity of man instead of morality in humanity leads to this clash between and among nations. As man misconstrues the principles between humanism and the church into one hybrid misinterpretation, conflict is assured. Tension and friction are measurable through modern history as acts of war and manifesting conflict solely produced by this malignant process of thought and understanding of self.

Nations align within the spectrum of this understanding as a fundamental ideological approach to governance and authority. Where *a* God is at the forefront of theocratic nations such as Iraq, Iran, Israel, Syria, Turkey, and many other countries in the middle east, the divinity of man is found more aggressively construed in nations like Russia, China, and the United States. Consequently, the three superpowers of the world. The irony in this as power corrupts absolutely without discrimination; power acts to legitimize the mind of the illegitimate. Not to say the governing bodies of these nations are illegitimate, but a shadow creeps into governance by human nature's subject to manipulation and to manipulation for personal prowess. Again, governance is not by the divinity of man when God is divine it is by the morality in man because man cannot be divine.

The irony lives in Ronald Regan's quote, "A nation that cannot *control* its border is not a nation at all." A fence between neighbors is not the possession or for the purpose of only one neighbor as obnoxiously loud and intrusive as one neighbor can be relative to the other. On individual and ideological principles, the neighbor's customs can be looked down upon in a reciprocal way. For one, a way of life is unusual if it is not familiar or contains ideologies comparative and complementary to the other. The act without the action of understanding from both parties spins the wheels of conflict. So yes, a nation that cannot control its border is not a nation at all. It is ironically based on the definition of how nations have become what they are through the lens of the scientific revolution. What did we say created nations? The intellectual border of understanding and not one from physical force and murky lines in the sand. Control is a funny word used properly in some contexts as well as improperly in another.

Protect, from a nation's point of view, would be to look out into the world from behind a wall. *Control* is to subject force, not from what is the same vantage point. Control is to go beyond the wall and prevent entry by force, whether intellectually or physically, through a funnel point to within. Control of a neighboring fence is dependent not on one or the other but on a compatible relationship to ensure its upkeep is met. At that point, *control* is attained not by one party or the other but by the cohesion of understanding between. If not, force nor intellectual independence or prowess nor any other attribute can maintain *control* because the residual effect of incoherence places a true line in the sand irrespective of any physical wall.

Where, though, is the border drawn between God and Man and goodwill and personal interest and free will as a controlling point or point of protection or inflection? Moving into the future of this document, we jump into modern world involvement between nations stemming from the scientific revolution to the current era and look into historical examples of conflict both against and within. The spectrum of measurement we described just above from divinity of god to divinity of man is illustrated through different points of time as a constantly swinging pendulum as cause and effect take its toll. Let's look into this clash of titans as the war between god and man.

Acts of War: Man vs. God

The hero of any story from mythology that links human interpretation as transcription from the heavens is a demigod. Part man. Part god. Perseus would behead Medusa and ride down from the sky upon Pegasus's back to slay the Kraken and save Queen Cassiopeia and the city of Argos. These stories are applicable pre-tensed in analogy as any act of goodwill by any individual or group of individuals against nefarious intent. Let us forget the awkwardness in Zeus' frivolity and note the polarity in good versus evil as Zeus battles Hades to control humanity. We should note that any act of aggression is not an act of goodwill, but that non-action is submission to ill intent. The term demigod only represents someone that looks both to God's divinity as it applies to man's morality and nothing else and not some sort of divine individual. That would be an oxymoron, wouldn't it, and against our spectrum to characterize the separation between. The moment one claims divinity as a man, they lose the divinity of god and cohesion to the pure morality of humanity. Morality is to know nothing. Divinity is to know all things. But, they continue to look through a Phantogram to see one perception split from two perspectives. One that sees the world in this way can kill the malignancy growing from manipulative practices of nurtured or nurturing subjects and slay the Kraken.

A hero's journey through a story is normally one individual descending into chaos to rise with a stronger will and understanding to defeat the antagonist. The story of the world is not the same but similar with additional complexities and deeper dimensions. The fight of man vs. god is not the normal dualistic storyline alluded to in most literary works as one versus the other but the individual's fight to remain centered along the spectrum of humanity and divinity to look both outward and inward simultaneously. The complexity lives in remaining central in their purpose instead of letting gravity pull them one way or the other. Perseus has a clear and imminent goal in defeating the Kraken. Humanity is not one individual, but the collective is measured as such and the sum of all collected individual averages. Humanity is the hero and belief in morality above one's self, not one actor.

The importance of extrapolating this complexity is to measure the hero of our story and understand the journey to victory. Gravity pulls our goodwill and intent or subversive actions one way or the other with every divergent choice that is made. Where Perseus, as a demigod, acts with a genetically coded will, humanity's will as the hero is sway-able along as a pendulum swings between Zeus and Hades. Why? Free will. Perseus acts without free will but the writer's will in one determinant path to defeating Hades. In this context, a closed genetically coded system with natural characteristics is given by the writer to dominate each choice, and nurturing is out of the equation. In the real world, the second variable is added, and further complexity is as well because we as human beings not divine in nature do not have the answer to *why*. Because, we do not, as human beings, in absolution, know the writer of reality's true intent.

In the context of our storyline, the earth and its population of living things should be thought of as one cellular entity fighting against an invasive virus from within or externally formed. Once we understand this, we can break our cell and divide it through mitosis. Cells fight against cells for domination, or they work together to replicate a cohesive understanding of mutually beneficial success. This leaves us outside or inside the castle walls of the nucleus and looking to each other as friends or foes. As we break our cellular body into multiple entities, we must continue to base our success on the laws of averages to determine if the cellular makeup of all of humanity as one will survive at any point in time. One large subgroup or metastasized cell charged by Hades and the Kraken can rewrite the story of Argos and sway the fate of humanity. Remember, as we continue, the additional variables added to humanity's story compared to a story written in ink. Free will and nurturing variables add enumerated complexities that can turn our hero or demigod into the villain outside the scope of a closed system storyline. Below we dive into war and head to the frontline.

Mitosis, The Civil War, and Cain and Abel

The year is 1861, and shots are fired on Fort Sumter in Charleston Harbor, South Carolina. The Civil War in the United States has begun. Our understanding of history is answered by the very simple questions brought into the complex of *who, what, where, why, when,* and *how.* The United States is at a divergent moment in history to align its identity with one or the other and not a mixture of both. Even though lingering residual effects persist, institutionalized recognition must align with one and not the other. President Lincoln acts to maintain the Union at all costs, whether slavery persists or is extinguished as the direct will of the people to whom he governs. Whether a noble approach or not, any leader must make the correct course of action for the benefit of all not one. At the will of the people, he does govern reliant on the divinity of God to lead and the morality of man to cohesively remain and reign authority.

The Civil War of the United States is our first example of a divergent path persisted by the misconstrued balance of divinity in man and subsequent mortality removed as Newton would say that for every positive, or action, there is an opposite negative, or equal, reaction. Against our law of averages within the United States in 1861, the movement away from homeostasis and into armed conflict has begun due in part to this balancing act sparked by the process of nurturing humanity has experienced. The luxury of a plantation owner for the inhumane acts against slaves directly correlated to removing that luxury is the cause of the civil war and the incapacitated cognitive ability to see slavery was an act of Hades in the first place that seeded its residual and fallout effect. The Kraken is released.

The trail leading to this point in history begins back to Mr. and Mrs. Caveman. Each choice along the way nurtured into a dissolution of cohesive intent and characteristics shared by now established Americans. Natural characteristics, of being 'Black' or 'White,' acerbated and accelerated divergence from the beginning of time and humanity to the brink of war as majority rule in authority outlawed all other variables against the average individual measurement of inalienable rights. Because one brother felt love and the other felt hate, divergence is inevitable, and friction creates fire. The first shot is fired.

The Union of the United States of America is a republic of one but the declaration of war and freeing of slaves created a mitotic separation of the American entity. One nucleus became two, and separate and conflicting cellular bodies are odds. Only one can exist in the space and time present in the United States at this point without killing the host entirely. The war is not between only the polarity in North and South but the strength of man's morality versus the strength in the illogical alignment with the divinity of man to act unjustifiably over another human being as God might. We are looking further into two entities at odds resulting from the dissolution of one state into two, scorching our path into applying the variables of ABi and $B\,In\,e$. We should remember this measurement is in relativistic terms and nothing else. Complete absolution is when both destroy the other. However, as energy is neither created nor destroyed, something remains whether in the construct of space or the space between two ideologies. As abolitionists act as the shield to protect the border between nuclei and confederates act to tear down the border between, we see the act to *protect* the free rights of all or one entity's fight to *control* the border between.

As Lincoln signs the Emancipation Proclamation, a pivotal and potent tool in accelerating the protection from and against authoritarian control, the goodwill and intent of the Union is established as the protector of freedom from invasive and arbitrary rule or control of humanity in North America. Without this declaration, unity of the Union behind one common goal and ideology is left unestablished, and therefore the physical "rallying of the troops'" is a potent concoction left unstirred. The thought of slaves joining to fight for their freedom is established in the institutional sense, willing and enabling them to pick up arms and defend their new freedoms under the morality of man but pre-declared and ordained under the divinity of God. An army of demigods against orcs and goblins is created. The force of ideology is backed and copacetically linked to the physical force of an army. An accelerant is created in potent form. One mass and density, which started as polar opposite but equal charge, begins to grow in strength against another. And so to look into the quantifiable measurement, in relativistic forms, of the ABi through the eyes of internal conflict.

Measuring ABi in Internal Conflict

The most interesting use of our *ABi* in characterizing the involvement between entities is found in mitotic cellular relationships of diverging and then converging nuclei dependent upon the result once friction is mitigated. We should realize a catastrophe to the proportions to which no remaining cellular entity has yet to occur. Whether we believe it or not is irrelevant because the simple observation is life itself is diligent and stubbornly committed to survival. That is not to say an event with absolute magnitude could not exist, but one to which all life ceases is unimaginably hard to concoct. Whether it is on this planet or the next, life will find a way. Not to step into the oddities and pessimistic realities of catastrophe, but just saying. We look at civil war within an entity as the ways a cell divides through mitosis, and then two separate and newly coded cells converging and fusing into one. Other processes we will describe in future examples of conflict and the end results are known as the Trojan Virus, Proxy Constant, and Super Bumpers. Noted are the effects that cause conflicts like these to remain in play or are extinguished into newly formed and institutionally recognized ideologies within an entity. Let's look at the figure below as we describe the Civil War of the United States.

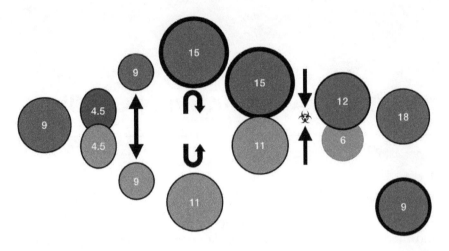

Noted are historical events and acts that work to positively or negatively accelerate the growth and density of each mass object as time persists. As tensions rise between North and South, complete divergence has not occurred until the Emancipation Proclamation. At this point, both entities are completely separate. Even though armed conflict is occurring, the peak of war has not broken out quite yet. Even if mass casualties are higher at this point it is irrelevant. Mass casualties in war are factored, but it is goodwill to overthrow ill intent that factors the relative state in each situation. The final battle, or turning point of the war, can simply be a duel between two people that turns the tide.

We should observe the points to which both entities, like boxers in a ring, diverge to their outermost barrier or corner in preparation for full-out assault with no regard for human life. This is when the rubber band and gravitational pull between growing mass objects is the strongest, and then suddenly they collide. Universes of thought and ideals clash like swords or fixed bayonets and muzzle blasts. The spiral of a new universe is created but from which one mass can be allowed to live or where one singularly dense point in the space of ultimate understanding and ideology remains until, of course, further conflict. As moons and comets crash and planets collide, new forms of mass are restructured. Just as the chemical makeup of one individual cell or the metallic and elemental properties of a planet or star are combined into one. Time and laws of gravity and space dictate what remains intact consumed into one dense ball spinning through time and what other particles are launched into the abyss left to roam without cohesiveness to any other component or ideology. For this, upon collision between entities carrying composited ideologies, slavery as the institutionalized act of forced physical labor in the Americas has left a comet roaming an empty vacuum.

The time between phase states depicts the point to which the freeing of slaves in the South both weakened the strength of southern States as well as strengthened and inversely accelerated the growth and density makeup of the Union. Just as the Earth is a planet of many resources and useful elemental products for cultivation and the moon or Mars is useless, a planet, or army, that consists of an array of demographics, nations, or beliefs tied under one flag always accelerates its density growth at a greater rate in an effort to sustain life and unity. Just as a plant or even a weed can't grow on the Moon, the extremely vast and balanced composition of Earth's elements allows for sustenance. In effect, the laws of nature dictate the laws in war but not of war. The imperative lies in a clash between entities and time between the assault and allowance of one entity or the other to build enough strength to dismantle the other. Just as life has its way like a stubborn way of existing, humanity is the same and ironically always on time. Just as Lincoln's declaration is imperative to the growth of the Union army, it is equally dissolvable of the Confederate's willingness to remain compatible.

Where secessionists are angered, abolitionists are equally but oppositely enamored. If the purity of darkness of one entity is to eradicate the light in another, an act must be strong enough to consume all light. If not, light always casts out darkness. As the light of emancipation is shined against the South, darkness is lost without a single bullet fired. Strength is absorbed by purpose, but soldiers are directly aligned to fight for freedom as an act against totalitarianism.

To look more in-depth at the figure, let's list our points of reference through time as accelerants for the Union Army or for Confederates as acts that add only to mass and density aligned or act to influence the accelerant of both. Here they are below:

Pre-Divergence: Confederates Succeed
From the Union: December 1860
Friction Kindling: First Shots Are Fired: April 1861
Divergence: Emancipation Proclamation: January 1863
Power Reduction: Reducing Accelerant Potency by
Destroying Access to Essential Infrastructure
Pivotal Clash: Battle of Gettysburg: July 1863
Gettysburg Address: November 1963
Establishing Final New Code: Circling Robert E Lee's Army
End of Conflict/Convergence: April 1965
Rebuilding Nuclei and Genetic Code: Reconstruction Era
Residual Effect: Jim Crow and Segregation

Confederate Army
Genetic Code - Ideology and Philosophy
Independence must remain for "Slave States" to
be "free" from Federal Non-Slave Law
Genetic Superiority is Established and must remain intact
Resistance to the removal of a commodity
that sustains the "way of life."

Accelerants
Plantation owners losing slaves to thoughts of freedom
and the negative impact on production
Robert E Lee as a vocal aggravator
Lincoln's Inauguration as a Potential Threat

Union Army
Genetic Code - Ideology and Philosophy
The Union and Constitution must remain to
Govern interstate law over individual states
Genetic Humanism is established and growing toward inalienable
rights, under God, granted by the Constitution of the United States.
Progress toward a new system of commodities
that creates a "way of life" for all.

Accelerants
Lincoln's Inauguration cohesive with Union principles
Frederick Douglas's vocal experience as a
Slave and for the rights of enslaved
Emancipation Proclamation as an un-equalizer
removing strength from the South.
Laws granting slaves freedom that fight for the Union Army

If we look at polarity charges in the diagram above, we can see the dominant polarity of positivity and negativity, but who is to decide which is which? Well, time does, and history decides through the perspective lens. Don't take this next sentence out of context, but there are always slight positive or negative charges present in each entity because neither are pure in their form, just as a concocted mixture within a cell. Every malignancy has grown within a healthy cell, and every healthy cell likely has a bacteria affecting its output but not entirely controlling it. If we look at both sides of the civil war to analyze which entity holds positive or negative dominance, we should break down the accelerants and genetic code inscribed within or transcribed in a Declaration of Secession or Constitution upheld and then philosophically.

Deductively, do the arguments for an action justify its intent to be acted upon if we looked at the Confederate argument to *maintain established economic principles*. Sure, it doesn't sound too bad, that is until you say maintain established economic principles of *commerce reliant on the subjugation and enslavement of an inferior race*. Hold up there. Abraham Lincoln just rolled in his grave. The justification contradicts the inalienable rights guaranteed in the founding document supported by the Union and by all other states. The first dimension of the argument didn't have anything wrong with it until clear characteristics were drawn. The Union's argument aligns with the Constitution, and the genetically coded argument and ideology states *all people born in the United States are citizens of this nation*. This is the 14th Amendment paving the way for a clash of ideas. The continued dimensional process then leads to all people born in the United States are citizens of this nation, therefore, *have the same rights regardless of color or creed*. The argument is copacetic in this, so that causes an effect upon institutionalized recognition that alters the current "way of life" for some.

A dimensional war in the North versus South theatre is played, and alignment with reality will always fall toward the positive charge. Why? Because the argument for and against based on the laws written in the 14th Amendment, whether it says *a pink cat can't swim if the pool is empty,* is valid in justification regardless of what the context says and aligns with reality and deductive reasoning unconsumed by emotion. Yes, a pink cat can't swim if the pool is empty is true. If the sentence reads simply, a pink cat can't swim, no cause is aligned with reason and remains absent of dimensional thought processing. Why can't the pink cat swim? If the pool is full and the pink cat can't swim, why not? Because they are genetically unable to? Or because pink cats can't swim in *this* pool? Deductive reasoning in conflict is lost for the most part but unavoidable if we are to defend against the control of an aggressor to protect those we are sworn to or unable to protect themselves. In the 14th Amendment, genetic equality through the eyes of God is established and maintained in time through the morality of man. Perseus defeats the Kraken.

The figure then represents a measurement of involvement and dominance of one entity over another. We must remember, our *ABi* and *B ln e* only measure the relationship between two parties at one static moment in time. The route in which AB is formed against the measurement of B is seen in the mitotic approach figured at the beginning of this subsection.

As AB is formed from the genetic code of B and by adding a new bacterial ideology, the two entities separate until space is no longer available in preventing or reducing the friction between them. Our accelerants act to embolden or enflame each involved entity until the distance is reduced to a frictional state and entities collide. The laws of nature then dictate, based on polar charges, which material components are to remain from AB and which are to remain from B. After divergence and then convergence, entity C is created. If we wanted to get super precise on every historical event to measure a quantifiable state of involvement, we would have to look into every battle, every shot fired, and down to every ounce of good or ill intent in everything from one plantation owner beating a slave for trying to flee to inalienable freedom and to every word uttered by freedmen in the North. Every glance of a supremacist is an emotional reaction, nurtured into them, against the simple genetic makeup of another human being as well as every submissive act by a slave in an act to prevent further harm to themselves or their family. Every single breath of goodwill or ill intent would need to be measured to have a completely precise measurement down to the atom of involvement between the North and South. That is unlikely and improbable, but a simpler measurement can explain the overall interaction between poles and summarized by well-noted and documented events in history. Let's take a look into a deeper level of the figures preceding this chapter.

Quantifying Figures

If we are to put relative figures to notable events throughout history, measurements can be found in analogy in applying acceleration to divergent and re-convergent paths of mass. With the figure above, let us apply these values to different phase states in the process of conflict:

	Phase 1	Phase 2	Phase 3	Phase 4	Phase 5	Phase 6	Phase 7	Phase 8
AB (-)	0	4.5	9	12	12	6	0	
i	0						0	
$z = (y - x)$	0	1.5	12	18	15	6	0	
$x = (r, d)$	0	3	3	6	6	3	0	
B (+)	9	4.5	9	18	18	12	18	9res
a	phi	0.5	1	3	3	2	phi	phi
$y = (r, d)$	6	3	3	9	9	6	9	3

In looking at our figures, we should note a in our ABi is not a definable term. The reason being, a is only a necessary measurement under $B \, ln$ because we again are working in relative terms, and the correlating comparison is then found in z, and the difference found in r, t, or both x and y. If we apply A in similar terms as $A\ ln$ instead, we look at the perspective of an event from A's point of view. Relativistic measurement only requires a accelerant to be a ratio for the acceleration of both A and B. We want to know at what rate B accelerates in terms of A. For this, an $a1$ and $a2$ are allowed to find the ratio of B's acceleration in terms of A.

Looking into our table of figures, i, as an integral figure depicts the moment friction occurs. In conflict, this is never a good thing but in shared ideology and goodwill, a combination of positive and compatible cohesion of ideals is always a good thing. We are not merely able to measure conflict but cohesion. Sure, one entity will always clash into another and become one, but that is not definable solely as conflict but resolution as well. Just as one army surrenders to another, two armies of goodwill can merge and disrupt the natural laws tied to the logic here. To understand the civil war as a conflict of ideas, look at the beginning y in respect to genetic code value B. When a mitotic relationship diverges into two reciprocating entities, our radius is always a higher ratio than our measured density encoded. Why? Because mass width lacks density. When ideas converge, and friction cools, density has a higher ratio *(phase 8)* as cohesion persists and denser and demographically new material is added. Sometimes when you don't agree with someone, or they sound uneducated and unwilling to meet you halfway, you call them "dense." That is, in this sense, incorrect use of the phrase. Density is actually a good thing. To insult someone that is unwilling to cooperate, you should say their argument "lacks density."

In symmetry and divergence, consistent ratio measurements are directly correlated with growth accelerant, mass, width, and overall growth. As an accelerant is added, a predictable growth rate and distance separation and consistent rate in separation is applied to the ratio of acceleration between both A and B universes.

Meaning, as accelerant is applied to mass B as a ratio of A and B's separate acceleration, the orbital path in separation is a consistent ratio. As B grows faster than A between phases 3 and 4, and mass is added to B, reciprocal separation is added to the relationship between where an accelerant only pushes A away without added mass and density. As a consistent ratio, the change in mass, again, as an accelerant is added, is to grow B and then grow the distance of A without affecting change upon the genetic makeup of A. The negative charge of ABi acts to propel against the gravitational forces of B instead of consuming an accelerant to grow. If our *a* ratio was inverted, the opposite would occur where universe A grows, and B is propelled outward as the distance is added between without growth and strength.

ABi Trajectory and Continued Orbital Path: Slope Relativistic Measurement

Accelerants and acceleration then are to push away or to grow mass within. The question left in the above table of figures is what about our *i* measurement? How do we accurately find this relativistic measurement of involvement between parties? The truth is, a level of measurement is always present if at any point a gravitational pulling power is applied. The mass itself could be measured as a physical mass with a pulling orbital pattern and path. To this note, we would see many different shapes than your normal sphere, a planetary object, or somewhat circular cellular body but more typical of your elliptical path and trajectory between masses that hold varying degrees of size and density. You should also think, in a vacuum vector of space, our measurement here is irrespective of any existing outward point of reference, meaning our path is plotted only as movement to or from. In this sense, our AB acts to move away as our B acts to grow, explained just above. For this, the path through time and space is then a spiral vortex where B has a destined point through the constant of time, and ABi orbits around this point of reference. If relativity were applied, the relationship between masses would center one path or trajectory through this vacuum.

The reason we do not apply this concept in its completeness and measurement using the Theories of Relativity is 1) complexity and 2) analogous instead of hard quantifiable data 3) to base the central movement through time and space as a reference of one to another instead of only between. To see the different points of view, we flip our measurements and apply A laws to B and flip *ABi* into *BAi* and then *B ln* to *A ln*. A relativistic central point of reference through the law of averages could then be applied. In more complex scenarios adding three or more universes of interaction, a matrix would need to be formed. In this scenario of adding a C universe, we get into the complexities of $ABCi$, ABi, ACi, BCi, $BC\ ln$, $C\ ln$, $B\ ln$, and other complexities. This would be in the event we did want to measure the involvement of superpowers in proxy wars or to break down the interaction of every single atom of every human being involved in production or destruction through involvement. The alphabet doesn't allow for that. Well, it does, but I don't want to type all of them in such a way to write this into the abyss of infinity.

So then back to i. As a measurement of true or false, there is always a measurement of gray between white and black and the hue that affects the overall composition of each entity. Where phases 3 and 4 would dictate a false narrative in this theatre of involvement, a very small true value brings these two mass objects back into involvement. Based on the ratios between mass and growth and separation, conflict will occur as an accelerant forces growth to outpace the pushing apart of each mass. At this point, the density and mass makeup of the dominant object forces interaction back into existence. For this, as it applies to the Civil War, the continued movement of military personnel as a response to the passing of laws and freeing of slaves acts to accelerate purpose, grow mass and density in purpose, and then catapult one entity into another. Space is reduced just as battle lines and front lines are formed as one mass collides with another. In the time between phase 6 and phase 7, as one mass dominates the other to consume its demographic components, the anaconda plan to corner and circle the Confederate Army and then March them to the Sea acts just the same as space and width of our $B\ ln$ mass grows and consumes the virus of ABi to cure an infection. However, residuals are not absent.

Residually, the material state of our new entity once phase 8 is complete is not left without prejudice that affects the genetic makeup of the whole. Just as new DNA nucleotide pairs zip, new component makeup is formed. Where a sequence may be read in Phase 1 as AT CG GC TA, the new sequence may begin to zip in the different form of CG GC AT TA. Cohesion remains principal in its fundamental structure, but the genetic code is altered. Residually, the entity through conflict is not unchanged. It remains intact after a divergent helicase breaks strands apart to pair with a new form until, of course, convergence is established, and the threat of a divergent historical event brings this process into play again and again and again.

Just as our entities are measured by the distance between and in a vector of space, x and y coordinates can be applied with z as a third plane. We must not forget, however, this is not where our dimensional process ends. When we invert and apply the process of understanding the relationship of entities as described just above in relativistic terms to chart a path between as opposed to a path in relation to, we can then dip into another form and perception. The Theory of Relativity is both adequate and inadequate in this observation in measuring the relationship between, but in its use, we forget the perception of each to compare the relative relationship each share from their point of view and instead only look at what is between. For this, the law of averages and Newton's Law is adequate but tedious in its computation to dip into the 4th plane of understanding and whisper to a 5th.

The residual left is grounded firmly, based on our cognitive understanding at this one static moment in time, between the morality of man and the divinity of God. When the dust settles and the last shot is fired, the moment of awe and levitation exists for a brief point left forgotten in history. When Union soldiers cheer in victory, truth in balance is at its peak. At this point, our entity is weightless but infinitely dense in its measurement and fights the laws of gravity itself. That is a brief moment of equilibrium established until the dust does drop and settle. For that moment in time, gravity acts to push just as much as it can pull. An accelerant of mass growth as a force of gravity itself is equal to the G constant of life in the meta.

We look into the residual as the after-the-fact effect upon the remaining entity and should find the beginning to understand the path to divergence and then rearrangement of genetic properties. Why do we use phi? Well, without it, nothing grows. Neither good nor bad can be born from a non-differential accelerant. If the ratio between entities remained one, then nothing would be created or destroyed or created to be destroyed. The differentiation and split are a bi-product of this ratio. Growth, as well as free will, must be a measurement left to the relationship between entities, or nothing new or free exists if the genetic coding of our entity and the universe itself was one and not phi, as the symmetry measurement in growth, the universe itself as well as all living things would, quite frankly, not exist at all. The coherence and cohesion of this concept allows life to exist. As small of a genetically encoded measurement as it may be, it matters. We would be beings, or cavemen, born on an uncharacteristically boring planet absent of any discernible features to absorb a nurtured effect from. Just as we are a product of our choices and a product of how we perceive the experiences we have, the naturally coded system in play allows for nurture to have the effect it does. If not, war would not exist, but neither would peace. The measurement in this chapter would be as boring as life on the moon when the Earth allows for growth through friction and conflict.

The purpose of our ln and e measurements are similar in regard to basing our foundation in phi. Even though we do not depict ln and e in the table above, they are constants in our measurement that allow for exponential growth. Because, as we know, through our understanding of phi and even into our understanding of Fibonacci, exponential growth applies to all matters of life. The properties of natural log and logarithmic functions are just that. What you give and what you receive is a never-ending sequence until the bulb of a plant is picked, and that form of life dies. However, through the natural laws of the Earth, it is likely, just as conflict acts to defend and attack or grow through decay, life will find its way for an entity to sprout again through the fruits of nutrition.

Multi-Proxy War and Internal Deception: A to Z

Looking into ABi, we do not stop when A and B cool the tension between and form a new residual state left as B^res. This new entity could be relabeled as C but unnecessary because as time goes on, a new measurement should be applied, and the root begins again to measure the relative juxtaposition between two entities where A and B are appropriate. We, however, do not end there. The completeness of our study, as we alluded to in the preceding sub-chapter, includes every atom and every molecule that we could sit in eternity to measure and count and write and never catch the full quantifiability of our model, for our understanding, though, we should dip into this thought.

From Algeria to Zimbabwe, the Continent of Africa is a melting pot for heat and, therefore, friction. We do not mean that solely on the placement along the equator, though the un-comfortability of dry and hot air adds to the tension against each and every individual if proper cooling, or AC, is not applied. The stress involved is almost a bi-product, both physically and metaphorically, of the atmosphere and environment. Populations require the simplest of forms to survive; water. And, so do crops. In this thought, the lack of this precious resource is detrimental to the individual as well as the whole. The presence of any other resource then is an accelerant for conflict because the fight is trivial if one or more groups wish to thrive. The triviality is in the cyclical nature of this continuing conflict and seen in the continent of Africa as civil war is a constant, never-ending battle, where progress toward peaceful relations is absent. The continental nation then remains divided without cohesion principles and only employs adhesive fundamentals.

When water splashes upon a mirror and a thin layer left, what happens more quickly than to a full pool of water? It dissipates, dries, without time to even evaporate. These molecules are not necessarily lost entirely, but adhesive principles in application act as a residual effect against the whole. When that thin layer adheres to a foreign entity or object and cohesion is not offered or sought over, the link between is only a thin layer of depth and inevitably dissipates without positively affecting the population as a whole from which that thin layer was separated from. What happens over time if you have one gallon of water in a contained system and you splash the entire contents upon a mirror and then collect what remains? And then once the layer dries, you splash the remaining contents upon the same mirror and let the layer dry? And then again and again still containing every molecule that remains? Inevitably, without the effects of evaporation, you are left with nothing. This is how we look at the negative residual effect of adhesive versus cohesive principles and the lens to which we will look at the multivariable and complex equation in terms of the continent of Africa in proxy wars and armed conflict that will lead to base our understanding against other forms of proxy war in the Middle East.

Africa's Multi-Variable Complexities

Remember as well we are not here offering an immediate solution to conflicts that have existed since the dawn of time for we do not have those answers yet. The natural response of any internet warrior is to assume they know more than the next person to which I will always say, in relative terms to the vastness of attainable knowledge, I know nothing but learn with every word. I could not tell you when I typed the first word of volume one that this next sentence would exist and how and where and when and why it would be a reference from and to, but I understand the way to which you follow a path lit for you. The path itself creates its own turns and forks in the road, presenting itself just as you think and create what is asked. The hope is to stumble upon a treasure at the end. And so we are here.

The complexity of Africa is probably one of the most elaborately complex scenarios present in the world today. Looking into complexities helps solve simpler problems and sheds light along the path to solve more multivariable and complex problems later along the journey. Every mathematical problem brought into the universe has a solution, whether or not you find it. We do not have solutions because we do not have that understanding in the meta involved with natural human relationships, both simple and complex, because emotion dominates logic. Logic, however, should not forget emotion as emotion is dependent on logic as a child is to his mother. Or, even, as nature is dependent on nurture in the growth of anything or anyone or any one nation or any one or more nations involved in the complexities of the world. The issue is when the mother becomes naturally dependent on a three-year-old for their own personal growth. At this point, the mother deteriorates, and the child does not grow either. As the thought applies to the continent of Africa, adhesive principles place the mother dependent upon sixty-one immature children of varying ages. I mean that respectfully in our analogy.

Included in this measurement are not only countries but disputed territories and states that no longer hold legitimate territories.

Sibling Rivalry

Algeria. Angola. Benin. Botswana. Burkina Faso. Burundi. Cameroon. The Canary Islands. Cape Verde. The Central African Republic. Ceuta. Chad. Comoros. Côte d'Ivoire. The Democratic Republic of the Congo. Djibouti. Egypt. Equatorial Guinea. Eritrea. Ethiopia. Gabon. Gambia. Ghana. Guinea. Guinea-Bissau. Kenya. Lesotho. Liberia. Libya. Madagascar. Madeira. Malawi. Mali. Mauritania. Mauritius. Mayotte. Melilla. Morocco. Mozambique. Namibia. Niger. Nigeria. The Republic of Congo. Reunion. Rwanda. Saint Helena. Sao Tome and Principe. Senegal. Seychelles. Sierra Leone. Somalia. South Africa. Sudan. Swaziland. Tanzania. Togo. Tunisia. Uganda. Western Sahara. Zambia. Zimbabwe.

As we dive into our understanding of the complex relationship within and without the African Union, we should establish a Trojan Proxy definition. A Trojan Proxy is not only a nation "doing another nation's dirty work." A proxy by our definition as it is applied is a state to which adhesive principle is applied, influencing the host nation. Where we normally see the term proxy applied is in terms of Turkey fighting Russia's war against the US in Iraq and Syria or many other forms. This is still true by our definition of proxy, but we are able to add to it another variable value. Proxy, by our given definition, is again any external effect for or against or in a manipulative way influencing the actions of a host nation. Where proxy is the act, a proctor is the actor as if the warriors within a wooden horse are a virus and the horse itself is the host carrier. Just as European nations influence the outcome of sovereign nations in Africa for their own personal benefit, we should note as well that personal benefit is sometimes also mutually inclusive and exclusive for the nation being involved. Even though democracy fails in large part in the continent of Africa based on genetic principles, it does act against the natural tendency to trend toward authoritarianism. The fault is then when democracy is a shade for personal benefit at the expense of the host nation, such as taking valuable resources the host nation already struggles over. To which this would be non-mutually exclusive.

To introduce the concepts of multi-variable entity involvement is to look at the curved spectrum between simple forms presented in *Volume 1* and then add another twist. Where a baseball pitcher can throw a fastball on a seemingly straight line relative to a curveball or slider is to look at the difference in adding a number of additional variables. The relationship between entities in a multi-variable setting, however, is not only the curve of the ball toward the catcher but the bending of the entire space to which the baseball travels to apply a new reference point between the pitcher and catcher. Granted, we may not see this when we watch the Giants versus the Dodgers, and we shouldn't because that is not the point of our reference. From the pitcher's point of view, there's only one trajectory point of reference, and from the catcher's point of view, the point of reference is similar in its singular measurement as the ball is caught.

However, what would need to happen for the pitcher to throw a ball in the opposite direction into the air toward the outfield and for it to hit the catcher's glove behind home plate? One of two things. 1) The ball travels all the way around the globe, but at this point, the ball would hit the back of the catcher, or 2) We manipulate the vector in which the baseball is traveling to alter the baseball's trajectory. As the ball thrown from the pitcher reaches its pinnacle height in its trajectory, center field and the center fielder would be inverted and now above the flight of the baseball and behind the catcher. The variable point of reference we must think about is the differentiation between reality and warped reality. To the ball, curving the vector of space in the outfield is non-variable, and the ball itself is unaware of any change. The ball ends up in its predetermined destination by virtue and still the law of physics though not laws we naturally understand. The pitcher essentially threw the baseball into a wormhole.

Big word. Wormhole. Our goal is not to establish the laws of physics to define and mathematically form the genetic properties of a wormhole unless by accident. Our purpose in this analogy is the descriptive measurements of multi-variables involved as well as involved by way of deception or cognitive dissonance that manipulate the relationship of cause and effect between multiple parties. It is easy to call balls and strikes between the pitcher and umpire's strike zone, but if we are to find the balance in all things with multiple proxy elements involved, then we must add more curve and spin to find a genetic state of equilibrium. Just as a nation is involved in the relationship between other nations, whether they are aware or not, balance is found in the field state left un-manipulated in its genetic properties. If in our measurement we find a nation throws a perfect strike, we don't need to bend space to make sure it gets to the catcher. If you made the pitcher shotgun a 6-pack, force him to spin 100 times around a bat on his forehead, and then turn off the stadium lights, the vector of space would almost positively need to be manipulated so the ball finds the catcher.

Oddly we find ourselves with a whirlwind of concepts of biology, planetary orbits, mythology, and now baseball. In our effort to explain the relationship between and among all nations in the continent of Africa and their proxy and proctor involvers, we should think back to the mother analogy of dependents and forces or nurturement in a family setting. Africa as the parent and the countries as her children can be thought of as a large family of dependent and immature children. Again, I use this term with no disrespect. Africa and her children live in a home, and the interaction all of her kids have affects the state of living in a home or just a house. Just like any family, compared to any other, you have siblings that fight and siblings that love to spend time with each other but still may fight every once in a while. You have families that disown their children or even, but very rarely, disown their parents for abuse or neglect and are removed from the equation by the state. The deciding factor that dictates this interconnected relationship is, of course, time, space, and the accelerant. "Time-out" and separation in space is an important disciplinary tool for a reason.

As we noted at the end of a previous chapter, positive and negative accelerants are either a resource or ideology or a combination. If we were to analogize a scenario within a family to further describe the relationship between siblings and this concept of interactions bending space-time, it would be along the spectrum of sibling rivalry. Let us form a scenario for analysis. Africa and her children live in a modest but comfortable home. All of her kids range in ages, as well as some have their favorites, and some have natural conflict. Africa's family, let's say, are naturally baseball fans, and some are pretty good at it. They enjoy getting a game together for those that are old and strong enough while the younglings watch and hangout. The problem we have is our baseball game only requires nine people on the field from each team at a time, and there is only one yard to play on and one baseball and bat with only just enough baseball gloves. At this point, friction is created because the space to host another baseball game is not available, and some are left out and have to wait their turn. What happens? Naturally immature and mature adults will have a different reaction to being left out or even from being able to join the game.

An adult that is able to play in the game realizes the recreational aspect and others being left out and may invite one of the less mature children to take their spot. Where adolescents can't decipher the emotion of inclusion or exclusion or just having to wait their turn, an adult can substitute themselves to accommodate the needs of others. The difficulty in this scenario is that friction between individuals is caused based on the number of immature entities and then multiplied and exacerbated based on the environmental conditions of space and time. Just as the scientific revolution "matured" the thought process of European nations, the requirement to build a sustainable system of governance in ideology and resource control must be present for a nation to mature. Sure, you can understand the entirety of the universe, but if you are not equipped to fly to the stars, you can't really say that you actually do.

The point being, Africa is a mature nation at heart but not in infrastructure based on the inability to obtain and maintain vital resource systems of control. Why? They just don't have the raw resources to do so in the environment present, and so friction within the family causes conflict that prevents growth toward sustainability. In the relationship between goodwill and intent, it is our pitcher, in analogy, that has control in which direction they throw the baseball. Are they aiming for the catcher's glove, or are they arbitrarily, by subversive action, trying to throw the ball into center field in the act of subconscious or conscious defiance. In our wormhole through time, how then can we measure intent, manipulation, and then measure a state of equilibrium differential that would depict how much vector curve is required if the baseball is to hit the catcher's glove. Again, balance in multivariable proxies is found when curving space and time is a non-requirement. If, however, pitch, trajectory, and inertia are away from our goal, we will see the present differentiation macro-molecularly microbic. Fun right? Absolutely. Even further, the risk in proctor power in inverted interpretation is the pitcher's assumption he is throwing strikes if in reality our trojan horse is bending reality to their will against equilibrium.

The Worm

Before we break down actual historical events up to modern-day relationships within and without the continent of Africa, we should establish first what and who acts as *the worm*. There is no wormhole without a worm to dig it, just as there is no black hole without a mole to burrow. Side note, neither are holes at all because that insinuates a hole can dig itself. I like the term "infinitesi-mole." Why? Because an infinitely dense point in time and space is not a hole but a product of something constantly digging. Anyway, let's think about *the worm* in this sense.

The requirement to bend space and time to fit our model is the result of the differentiation from a state of equilibrium as we bring multi-variable proxies into play. A wormhole is naturally defined as bending the space between two points in time or vice versus bending time between two points in space. In our thoughts of proxy relationships, this is a measurement solely based on the causal relationship between the pitcher and catcher as the dominant and dependent. A catcher doesn't know exactly the pitcher's intent until the ball is in the air and dependent on them throwing the ball in the catcher's general direction. Just in this way, the environment and relationship between cause and effect from nurturement factors can manipulate the intent of mature or immature entities. The characteristics of the previous sentence are defined then as the worm.

Any deviation from proxy influence or natural internal factors that cause the differentiation between two or more entities requiring the bending of time and space to reach a common goal is the worm that forces manipulation. Because our accelerants are ideology and resource control, proxies and proctors have incentives effectible upon, against, and for the same accelerants or accelerant control. This again is the curve of a curve because involvement is discernible and decided within the same theater of time and space but adding more than one perception upon the stage referenced against the same point in space-time. Where diamond fields in Botswana are a resource to its people, the influence of an outside agent or proctor nation-state creates a manipulative cause and effect against the miners in Botswana. For example, miners dig for diamonds they think are only being sold for the profit of Botswana, but in the shadows, a European nation is actually spinning the process to where complementary profit is absorbed for their substituted benefit. Again now, mutually beneficial or not? If exclusion or inclusion is followed along compatible lines, no manipulation in space and time is required, but in the insidiousness present, massive amounts of curvature against reality are required to maintain the status quo until the threshold reaches a catastrophic breaking point. You can only manipulate something or someone until they become fully aware. The worm then is not only the proctor but the cause and effect from both sides of the equation that set the stage to bend reality around two or more goals differing from involved entities around one point of assumed control.

Three Points of Reference: Bending the Border

In measuring the relationship between nations in Africa, we pull three points in time for each measurement. Of course, there is no way to outline every moment in history for a very real and quantifiable measurement, nor are we able to involve every single nation in this section because, again, I do want to finish this book at some point and not write into eternity. But we will do our best to encapsulate the thought of infinity into a bottle and toss it to the sea. Three points of reference in the relationship between involved nations are then to be used to look into our historical events.

Before we get into the history of development or non-development of the African continent, we should first lay our definitive terms. Accelerants such as ideology or resource control from the modern colonization period of the 19th and early 20th centuries have a few common characteristics beginning to spin faster and faster in their complexity. In the 19th century, European nations and even natives of the continent began to grasp their foothold of control without much grip. As a burning oil loosening the grip of peace entirely, we have two common features as resources with value 1) Oil Fields and 2) Uranium mines. The importance of Uranium is not quite thought of in the minds of superpowers at this point because superpowers today were only building a foundation to this point in time where muskets and bayonets were a measure of power against bows, arrows, and spears. Uranium enrichment is not yet founded as an intimidation through the threat of force.

The friction in the continent of Africa at a point in time where the rest of the world was becoming enlightened to new sciences and ways of life prevented the full maturity and development of Africa. As European nations were creating new forms of technology, African natives were still becoming African Americans and shipped across the ocean. Manpower as the number one resource is removed. The ability to create a home of their own within Africa, we discussed previously as a direct cause of the Civil War in the United States, is prevented by the proxy force to build someone else's.

As we jump through our points of reference and overall look into conflict as we began by diving into the United States Civil War, we will sandwich two large conflicts together and jump back and forth between them. These being World War II and the Cold War with cause and effects of before, between, and after. As the colonization of Africa became a front for proxy influence, the spin rate of space manipulation increased by the day and hour. Where very black and white terms of resource control are present pre-World War II, the manipulation of time and space is ever so prevalent during the Cold War and even thereafter. Where the simplicity of Britain and France's sprint to control the Nile access was merely to control the pathways of trade into East Asia of simple commodities just wait until oil is a monetarily valuable resource and uranium disintegrates inhabitants of Japan.

Our points of reference are just this. The declaration is irrelevant between accelerants as ideology or attainable resources, but we can define one as time and the other as space. For simplicity, let us just say ideology is time and resource control is space. As the spectrum of ideology expands into Marxism and communism or free enterprise and capitalism, our reality in the theatre of African conflict is manipulated. The cut and dry *this is mine*, and *that yours* is evidently absent when colonists declare borders between European nations that native inhabitants have no acknowledgment of. The depiction is left then in the differentiation of this physical but metaphorical line in the sand between *what is* and *what is as well* but through a different lens affecting inhabitants as a cause of dominant and manipulative tactics against the subversive. The difference of views against one object over time and exacerbated potency of accelerants causes incredibly unstable and unsolvable friction points of reference. Imagine two or more children fighting over who gets to play with a toy car and be in the driver's seat if they aren't playing with a car at all but a remote-controlled boat.

A dispute is formed about who can drive the car down the road the best and safest, but in reality, they are moving their toy down a stream. Reality is lost, but not in the sphere of those that are deeply involved in first person. Just as we only understand what the color blue is because someone once told us but who knows what that hue looks like through the lens of the other. We never know what another sees because when you pick up a Crayola crayon, it simply says blue even if the hue is not the same as another sees it. They grew up their entire life knowing the color of the crayon is also Blue, but no comparison is ever able to be found.

Reality in a proxy war is not what you think it is if you are a proxy or proctor in it. Just as Cold War superpowers influence the lives of natives thousands of miles away from the comfort of an office building, or by spies among us, life on the ground is incredibly different. Where one person is robbed of the ability to pay for essential resources by their job at a Uranium mine before the proper enrichment of a reactive and raw resource, another sees bolstering their strategy as a threat of and through nuclear proliferation. We inevitably will see that the dominant proctor will always negatively impact the proxy even if the promise of gold and silver is guaranteed. Why? Residual effects will inevitably act with promise of radioactive fallout. I mean that both metaphorically and literally if the accelerant resource is indeed uranium deposits. You may not see it immediately, but the crumbling of society, by the grip of control against a reciprocal effort to protect from barbaric and military coups and heated conflict, will always be present if a threshold of balance is never met. The quagmire is built. An infinitesi-mole is digging.

As we look into our events of conflict, let's outline our accelerating points of reference to look back to as we write and ride into the past.

Point One: Pre-World War II / Imperialism and Colonization
Time: Ideology of Physical Rule and Territory Residency
Space: Resource Control of Raw Material
Mines and Channels of Trade
(Ivory & Rubber)

Point Two: During and Post World War II
/ Pre-Cold War Tension Mounts
Time: Ideology of Governance through Lens of
Free Market or Communist Establishment
Space: Resource Observation of Enriched Material
and Increased Value of Oil Fields
Point Three: Cold War and Post-Cold War
/ Superpowers Super-Feeding
Time: Ideology of Market Systems and Independence
From Oppression / Communism as a Threat
Space: Commodity Value Peaks and Leaks into
Neighboring Countries and Continents

Imagine proxy conflict and interpretation of what science and physics measure, as the figure below. Those who write history depict one curve in reality, but a second curve from a separate and equal perspective balances our equation. Just as if we look to the moon blocking the sun during a solar eclipse to see gravitational waves manipulating space, the sun has a perspective as well. Not only one viewpoint should be referenced, whether a winner or loser in war or in history. Contemplated should always be both sides of a spectrum to see what is right in the middle. The proctor always shapes reality understood through the proxied and then inversely perceived, whether that is from the viewpoint on Earth or from the Sun.

Before the Turn: 19ᵗʰ Century Internal Conflict

By definition, a war between inhabitants of Chad and Nigeria is not like an actor in a theatre of civil war if you look at it as one country against another. Because a federal-state system is not present, it simply appears as a civil war without official decree. The lack of governing principles of grouped nations is a cause for war and more unrest when questions of ownership are not met with answers from an African United approach. Though Africa itself is then not a country, civil war is not the correct definition, but it is the true one. Reason being, the mother nation and her children. A theatre set within Africa, in this time period, is just as the United States was 200 years earlier, except conquistadores have modern weaponry and scientific knowledge in relative terms to natives. Instead of acting under the flag of "Conquest," we just painted the pig a different color and called them Imperialists; because we are intellectuals, not barbarians. However, external aggression over internal control of African nations and resources is the same just 200 years later with a handful of words added to the dictionary and hundreds of books written with them. The "end always justifies the means," but in reality, prejudice is what is left.

The Road to Borno, Nigeria, in the late 19ᵗʰ century is where we begin with Lieutenant Rabih and his army fighting both native inhabitants as well as the French. The first proxy was well ahead and rested in time. Even though France was present in Africa many years prior, we look at the turn of the century for context. The term *Francafrique* is used to define not only territories but ideologies within the sphere of French control during colonization. And this is just it. France is present in Sub-Saharan Africa for the promise of civilization improvements by government decree but trust when we say absolute power corrupts absolutely and never trust when they say we are from the government and are here to help. What was lacking for the benefit of native inhabitants was surely reciprocated by pillage.

The purpose is spun in reference to two points of view over one resource, land. Control of trade routes and economic exploitation is what ensues in any and all residency of a foreign power in a submissive and underdeveloped nation. Just as we will see during and after the

Cold War, the small-powered entity is always drained to bolster and strengthen the dominant power to become more dominant. The simple concept in *Volume 1* of human nature to be advantageous is not absent when we speak of countries or nations. It is actually much, much worse. The exponentially rising value of production can increase with collective collaboration, but so can destruction. Opportunity is never lost in any one opportune moment. Just as the Kraken or Hades is fueled by the absence of peace or goodwill, so is a proctor nation under a flag smeared by intent.

France and local natives at odds with Rabih were met with force and fury that outweighed modern warfare but only for a short period. French diplomats and other allied nations and kings were overthrown and beheaded or imprisoned during this period until just after the turn of the century where spears and arrows were simply just not enough. As a nation is starved and dehydrated from constant war, defensive power and aggression can only lose its power and luster. Rabih and his heir are eventually overthrown as the militarily legitimized governing authority. This, of course, is not even close to the end of military rule. Even as weaponry slowly increases through technological advancement, barbarian rule in Africa remains, and force is still the equalizer when progression normally is paced and paired with intellectualism. Weaponry advancement thus is a non-factor. A nation involved in constant conflict, even if its weaponry evolves from wood finished to bronze, simply does not have the time to focus on construction. A nation squeezed of resources has nothing to fuel the melting pot of renaissance and smith a new ideology when all they know through time and space is conflict and not peace or positive collaboration. The state remains. The accelerants become potent. Spin accelerates the exponential differentiation through and between collaborative realities. In this case, they are speeding up the consensus reality of time associated perceptions.

Time Dilation is the warping of space and affects an object present within the sphere of dilation to rapidly slow the aging process or, in relative terms, speed the aging process of an observer outside the frame of reference. Looking into this process of thought brings us into the genetic and physical properties of how we understand the universe through an infinitesi-mole. What then is our frame of reference, and who then resides within or without the sphere of dilation? I can tell you one simple thing. How does time feel when you are angry or fearful for your life, and how does it feel when you look into the eyes of the person you love? Fast or slow, but the point of reference is odd in this sense. Just as we get confused when we turn the clocks back but the sun essentially moves forward relative to the tick-tock of a clock.

The truth and reality are, the sun doesn't care and shines without any frame of reference, but our perception of time is diluted by our exceptions tied to a clock. For this, as the dual observation principle would back, the invention of a clock is our faulty approach in controlling the sun that orbits around our lives. When you woke up late after springing clocks forward, how did you feel the moment your body woke up thinking you were late for work? Time was fast, but you were slow. How do you feel when you woke up and realized you had an extra hour of sleep? Time was slow, but you were fast. The relationship between you as a measurement within a vector of space and the vector itself is then manipulated by the interpretation of your movement through that vector. Through deductive reasoning, you, as a vector, assume at the same time dilation properties subject then to manipulation.

My point being here, as France occupies and controls a small territory within Sub-Saharan Africa, but the large majority of its power lives thousands of millions away though mountainous enough to cast a shadow of power, the object point of reference is manipulated through proxy involvement. A proctor has the ability then to manipulate how both the collective and all individuals within the collective view reality. When a resource is trivial to a superpower as a luxury but a requirement for the survival of a submissive nation, how is time looked through the spatial lens of each? To France, perhaps they simply get a bad reputation. For the Congolese natives, death steps closer to their door. The difference is immensely under-evaluated in the relative relationship between all proxies and proctors of civil or nation-to-nation conflict. Just as our modern world has provided us with luxurious technological advancements to make life easier, we think the world is ending when our phone dies. As a positive accelerant to "bring people together" but a subsequent potency to "push people further apart," technology has the same effect. Imagine the difficulties felt by an adolescent youth in 2021 that their parents won't buy them a car when they turn sixteen, and they feel the world is unfair but refuse to put themselves in the shoes of a child that survived Hiroshima or the Blitz of London or Paris. Some adolescent youth throughout the world do not demand a car from their parents but only hope the one they are walking by does not explode and kill their entire family.

The differentiation between spatial recognition between realities is clear as day, causing great highs but massive lows. Tragedy is an everyday thing where we are shocked to hear the news of something so abhorrent and then simply go about our lives agitated by our phone's battery not lasting long enough to read that abhorrent news. For this spin is added, and the world's perception of reality begins to swing higher but lower between what is real and what is a fallacy. Perhaps one day, the swing ends, or someone comes along with the bright idea to bend space around two swinging adults that act like children, enough to make their accelerated focus equivalent and remove its negative affectability. This again is depicted in the bending between two perceptions in the figure just previously illustrated, as well as the dimensional circle to spheres below.

Start to Spin: French and European Descent and Departure

As we descend into the construct of dilation between the observed and the observer, we continue to monitor the effect of proctors to manipulate not only the conscious experience but this reality before, during, and after civil conflict. The continued manipulation of viewpoint perception and manipulation of resource control is then investigated.

As, nothing that increases in mass and spin rate remains the same or stationary without growth or decay through new genetic additions or malignant threat to the host—looking into reference point analogy in an uncertainty principle found in the hair of Einstein. No, I do not mean the mop on his head but the hairs of his findings. Theoretical physics and mathematics applied to the Theory of Relativity suggest infinitesi-moles do not have hairs classified in the no-hair theorem while Stephen Hawking suggests otherwise. So True or false? Funny that you ask as I answer my own question in between second and third person. This depends on the dilation concepts in the preceding chapter, if you are an external observer or internally observed or an internal observer or externally observed. That is the fundamental of Relativity in itself. As a train moves, the only valid perceptions are reference points between A and B to measure the space and time between. As a train moves, speed is measured by the observer's relationship between a power pole and the mountain landscape in the distance. If the power pole, or the mountainside, were cognitively aware, they would match their interpretation of the same measurement in different contexts.

How in a heck of Hades does this matter in the constructs of the Horn of Africa? Another great question, thank you for asking. Ever have ingrown hair? They suck. In a purely theoretical approach with no basis in calculation, we can still set a hypothesis. What if infinitesi-moles are like a nasty mole on your face but one that burrows, has a hair or two? The answer will be discussed when we get to modern conflicts in Iraq, but we'll leak some of our mass and coding beyond the horizon leading up to that section.

Turn of the
century

Pre WWII
Increased
Acceleration

Cold War Proxy
Spin Increases

Francafrique

Aw yes, the "sphere of influence" of France within the continent of Africa. One observation, two questions. Observation being: Don't spheres take oddly round and planetary shape or planets take spherical shape? They sure do. Question: What does this sphere do as it pulls and pushes its ideology? Question: Where and when does this take place in time and space? The observation leading to the default logic behind answering our two questions is the analysis forthcoming.

Francafrique is a term coined during the Cold War but a coin smelted much earlier in history in preparation for cashing in. France's involvement in Africa is noted in the previous referral point of context as clashing with natives during the end of the 19th century and even earlier into the late-mid 19th century. After the turn, and before the first World War, resource control's imperativeness as a potent accelerator is centered around the concept to control what was not yet understood. Uranium mines were not a crucial detriment to society but a kryptonite of monetary value yet to be discovered. The establishment and tactic was and is to maintain connected routes through territories at the cost of anyone else with the ideological shadow of a proctor there to help inhabitants. Examples are the Saint-Louis-Dakar and Dakar-Niger railways connecting inter Sub-Saharan African to the West Coast. The dream, as it will come to fruition during the Scramble for Africa of European Imperialists, would then be to reach all the way to the Nile and the Red Sea and maintain dominance of supply routes.

This project enabled France to connect land and sea and transverse rugged jungle terrain from the ports of Dakar to the expanse of the Niger River that snakes through central Africa, allowing supply boats to drop raw resources to then ship out to the rest of the world. The tough deal is claiming someone or something is there to help, and if inhabitants don't want their help, they help themselves anyways, and inhabitants are expensed to the budget's bottom line. It sounds like a rotten process of thought of an insecure little man but happens every day in trillions of encounters, and even if agreed upon, the residual fallout remains a guaranteed, no-money-back inevitability.

The relationship between the Saint-Louis-Dakar and Dakar-Niger railways and other new advanced forms of transportation depicts the residual fallout even if a conflict is avoided. Though a planetary object may not crash into the mass of another meta-celestial body, that does not mean the effect is absent. Just as an anomaly can absorb and suck dry the nutrients and enriched material of an object through gravitational force into a singular dense point in time, so can a proctor over a proxy. As the Saint-Louis-Dakar railway became an inconvenient way of transporting goods across the globe, the same inconvenience is then expensed upon the host just as a child leaving the dinner table without cleaning their plate and putting it away. They sure did, however, eat all their food. The ports and stations along the railway diminished and slowly deteriorated the cities and towns within their "sphere of influence." French bases and military personnel began to move to other parts of the world and with it their protection, as an established entity, of the influenced inhabitants. Civil war for control is now opportune, and physical force is present as an advantageous approach to place authoritative power upon submissive and newly poverty-stricken civilians. Even as the benefit for the people within their sphere was present, and the pitcher was throwing strikes, clean removal of dependent commodities opens the door for manipulation like a drunkard coming in to close a one-run game. He could be an angry drunk or a happy drunk, but the truth is coordination is still lost and objective with it.

A not so loving and abusive father or mother bent on addiction and consumption at the expense of their dependents and subordinates would act quite differently. Unjustifiable or skewed justifiability for abuse is always the reason a parental figure scapegoats blame for personal failure against a dependent, "If you never were born!" Up until this point, the potency of consumption is a watered-down beverage relative to increased toxicity and alcohol proof and percentage within our accelerant. For drunkards, they are usually pleasant people if they are not consuming. Or if they are between benders, they typically act with malice but not excessive or with no end in sight. Typically anger is derived from the between points of going up and coming down. When a drunkard is subject to alcoholism, they say it "only takes one drink," and then the train is headed off the rails until a crash and recycling of the process. From sobriety to consumption to rage, the path is predestined based on potency or sorosis. The way in which we look into this process can be subjugated against moderately peaceful plunder of resources through a somewhat cognitively deceptive tactic or the all-out aggressive path to resource control. One is usually by physical force and the other by intellectual prowess not yet met by resistance.

How the French garnered control over the supply chain from Africa out into the rest of the world is the way in which a drunkard retreats from their bender. Aggression tactics before are not necessarily washed clean from reason or removed from optional tactics, but the validity in their reasoning is to retreat from a substance they depend on and substitute something else into their psychological justification of being. Even though alcohol suppresses emotion, it does not eliminate them. On the comedown, usually, a re-justification of being is present to calm or filter suppressed emotion into an introverted perspective. The hate for all things inflamed by potency and flammable concoction during or the justification for loving all things substitutes their hate but without a basis in reality. Normally, one finds God in this path. Whether that is justifiable or not, I will leave that up to the individual, but the analogy is, "they found God until when?" It only takes one drink, and then hate and anger substitutes their love for all things. The truth is, in genuine enlightenment of greater power, that one drink is never consumed, and the exponentially inflated sense of God is watered down but not absolved. This is indeed where God does exist, turning "wine into water." The dissolution of an inflated sense of power and connection to it is watered into their life as opposed to drowning them in it. One becomes incapacitated by the thought of God just as they can be by the flip of a shot glass, and negative effects are seen as residual. If one is so infatuated with a higher power, it incapacitates their ability to think rationally and they are still a drunkard. God is found in the calm of the middle, not in the swinging of a see-saw. One that is consumed by wine or drowned in water is unable to float along the surface.

The use of intellectualism as justification to replace the use of force and abuse begins as conflicts between parties are suppressed but not removed. Just as the physical threat of assault is absent in our analysis of the Saint-Louis-Niger railway and France's exit, the intellectual justification drowns the remaining inhabitants in poverty. The consumption of resources through intoxicative principles in polarity is still present. The spectrum of entities along the snaking of railways through mountainous terrain is our line of proxied nations affected by the chain reactions subjected by our proctor nation. Our figures below depict the calm and semi-conflict free, in relative terms, of resource intoxication.

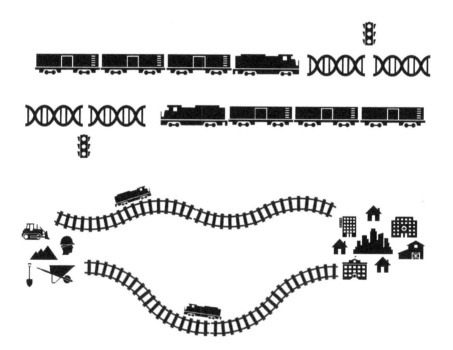

All Aboard!

Real events in the history of Africa involved railways as territory transit and means of control. Resource movement, in the time before reliable roadways and massive cargo ships or even pipelines, relied on a system of railways. Movement, from point A to point B, is then able to be manipulated through curvature. As the worms in our previous analogies, control of railway tracks is just the same. The irony, in our study that includes the strands of DNA, is that train tracks depict the bonds of polypeptides much more than we may think. Similar to the rungs of a ladder, movement through time is substantiated on the ability to move from point one to two. Whether that is vertical or horizontal, the link between two parallel lines allows for locomotion.

Each railroad tie is then equatable to each set of nucleic base pairs. As time persists, or a train is in motion, what happens if a set of railroad ties becomes disjointed? The same thing if a segment DNA is unmatched in pairing bases, collapse, stop codon, or a massive railway catastrophe affecting those within proximal location. The physical setting of pairs as replication occurs may be microscopic but the analogy is the same. As one strand offers a nucleotide to the other, our train moves another tie down the track. Balance and maintenance of our railway, just as polarity in pairing must be maintained, is imperative.

The issue we have then is when maintenance of reality is not kept. The bending and shaping of perception in proxy involvement weighs against the tracks as freight load is added but not factored in upkeep. Maintenance of our rail cars and engine must be kept just the same. The balance between resource attainment, removal and input through production systems is then a variable in computation. A simple system, seen above, is when resources go directly to inhabitants without divergence from delivery. The same engine and rail cars then return to pick up another load. Reality is based on truth. A proctor nation is non-variable against inhabitant villages or industry sectors. The problem is when divergence adds movement north removing input from movement west to east.

Next Stop: The North Pole

A divergent path, or in biological terms in replication and transcription, is a helicase wedging apart replicating strands of DNA. If divergence is factored an equal convergence variable must be added on the tail end. This requires a ligase to realign pairing strands and paths. We should, however, note even if divergence equals convergence, reality is manipulated and affects the relationship to reality between proxy and proctor. If the movement to and from is balanced as a 1-to-1 ration, absent of diverging and converging events, involvement to and from will remain unaffected from outside influence. This is what we see in our figure here.

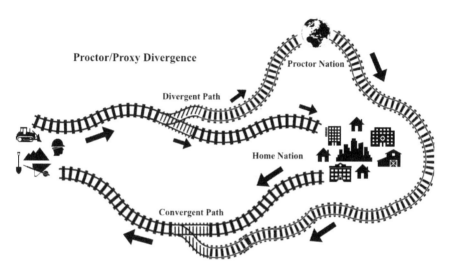

Though, in Africa, this is not the case. Every act of divergence removes from our 1-to-1 relationship of input to output and margin of differentiation if felt between proctor and proxy. Perhaps our divergent ratio removes 0.5 but converges another 0.5 upon return. This does nothing for the proxied nation. Why? After divergence, our freight train headed to the north pole and bypassed inhabitant villages to deposit positive energy. Positive energy was then only routed after convergence to increase raw material extraction. In the cascading effect we see in the use of rail systems of the western edge just south of the Sahara, each act of divergence increases with each shipment as inhabitants do not realize the true effect.

Our 1-to-1 ratio of interpreted reality is actually 0.5-to-0.5. Inhabitants still function as if a 1-to-1 relationship exists, manipulating our vector of space and time. We do not fully see nor feel our nucleotides breaking apart until production halts and our cell body is left unresponsive. Villages along the railways suffer upon expected shipments that never arrive. Maintenance is required but energy input is unfeasible due to bypassed potential energy. Sooner, rather than later, a new form of locomotion is established and instead of using the tracks between point A and B, our bypass is now the main route from A to C. Station B is no longer a stop along the way. Energy potential is depleted and actual energy is suffocated into nothingness. A 0-to-0 relationship between A and B is established. Absolution along our segmented line is the result in warping reality beyond correction. The residual effect is felt only by proxy nation B and their inhabitants.

Anger and Abuse in the Relationship Between Nations: Santa's Problem

As the world works through World War I, France is increasing abusive conflict within the continent of Africa as a dominant entity over a dependent nation. In this role, Africa should be noted as a dependent, not on their own terms or will. As proxies and proctors manipulate the scope of reality and thwart the space and time between, the reason is given, but reason is not achieved. Africa is indeed an independent nation where the justification of maintaining their dependency is almost a nice way of blackmailing someone or shaming them into a relationship. The "if you don't do this, I will do this" approach is not a beneficial action of mutual inclusiveness. Instead, it is a dark look upon Santa and the North Pole with all of his worker elves. Santa is by all intent and purpose a great childhood experience, but we are about to throw a shade of darkness against it. Prepare. This is not how I look at or think of Santa in the normal context because I enjoyed Christmas very much as a kid. Don't think this analogy is my natural thought of Santa. He's a great guy. We met when I went to Switzerland last year and jumped up into the Arctic. Mrs. Claus is a treat as well.

Imagine a scenario where Santa needs to get the most out of his elves because production demand is high this Christmas, and not enough toys have been made for all the semi-deserving kids out there. He needs to do something and will do anything in his power at any cost to ensure the deadline of Christmas Eve is met, and all the toys are ready to be dropped off. Santa gets this idea from the Nazis that Crystal Meth is a great product to ramp up the heart rate and speed up production, so what he does is spikes all the cookies the elves eat before their day. Production is doubled within a week, and the deadline is certainly to be met. However, Santa has a problem. There is one rogue Elf that found Santa's stash and has created a small gang of elves to hide out by a dumpster behind the toy shop after work. Santa confronts Elf, where Elf blackmails him in a way in which Santa's secret will be told to all the elves if he tries to punish him. Now, the power of Santa is questioned, and gang war is almost guaranteed. Sooner rather than later, some elves begin to overdose, and people begin to ask questions. At this point, Christmas Eve approaches, and Santa loads up his sleigh. Being aware of the inevitable revolt by the north elvish gang, Santa takes Mrs. Claus with him and never returns to the North Pole after dropping off all the semi-deserving kids' toys. Instead, he heads back to the parliamentary quarters in Europe.

ELF Aquitaine

The darkness of the analogy is hopeful to not scare children that wish for Santa to send them toys but has its reasoning in structure. ELF is a French Oil Company involved in conflict in Africa during colonization and imperialism attempts to maintain control of both resource and ideology accelerants within the Sub-Saharan region. As the Industrial Revolution as well as World War I increases demand and monetary value for commodities, the number one resource with peaked value is, of course, a commodity we fight over to this day, oil. During this period in time, and with structuring faults in the foundation of French involvement in Africa on official decree, France was unable to maintain control and legitimacy both in the Sub Sahara as well as at home.

Conflicts begin to arise based on absent legitimacy and the decay of the curtain of fallacy. Where the benefits of oil extraction were promised to benefit the inhabitants, the benefit of massive wealth sniffed with toxicity and taste. A drunkard had his one drink. Independent from the laws of France, the privately-owned oil company was consumed and intoxicated by greenbacks. Incentive and purpose were removed entirely from the storyline sold based solely on the genetically coded framework of involvement when France entered the continent. French law, dictated on foreign soil, and the process to which this "aid" was funded left a gap in budgetary reconciliation. French nationalists and imperialists working under the pig-painted guise, of the state to the state but for their own profit internally, created our differentiation between realities.

Our players in this scenario are 1) African Inhabitants 2) Civilians in France 3) French Representatives Aware and Benefiting 4) French Representatives that are Not Aware and 5) French Imperialists on the Ground. The African Inhabitants in our measurement of spatial contortion are not even aware of groups 3 or 4, which causes disruption in understanding the real perception of group 5. What they see are simply French Representatives. As Imperialists begin to pay the inhabitant government to maintain control to subvert revolt and aggression from civilians, tension only mounts, and emotions are suppressed. Again, suppression never removes what is inevitable to rise. Ideology as a resource is beneficial for this suppression because being two hundred years behind the advancements of the scientific revolution makes democracy two hundred years in the future and a concept foreign in practice. It is simply easy to suppress the morality of man if morality is not a word in the dictionary or if libraries do not have books readily available. Regression into conflict is the only route from here. As tension rises and France's occupation continues, the noticeable absence of "benefit from promised resources" is seen, felt, and inflamed by the people who are promised something and get nothing. When the books don't balance, someone in an intellectually driven society knocks on your door and asks, tells, and then throws you in jail, but for one that has not experienced the enlightenment era, they simply cut your head off. Good elves are coming for Santa and the North Elf gang flees as well.

Remaining European Imperialism: Scramble and Scrabble

France is noted as a largely integral factor against the evolution of the African state of states. We, however, understand the nature of any growth into maturity and the growth of an ally to the United States through many examples of cooperation for the common good. No nation involved in a foreign territory is immune from the negative causal relationship between them and the involved entity. We, as human beings as individuals or as collections of individuals, look to our self-interest. It is simply human nature. There is not one example in human history of occupation that a proxy nation did not have any negative effects felt by the residency of another nation. The effort of expansion will always show a residual effect. Growth will always devour the old and replace the old with the new. There is no avoidable path to growth without consumption. Our goal then is to limit residual impact upon the inhabitants of a nation in a newfoundland.

The truth is the truth. Perhaps in attempting to sign a deal with a publisher largely based in France, the preceding subchapter risks the logistics of such a deal. But, again, no one is immune. If we do not like history, it is not to wipe it clean and punish or manipulate the perception of it but to know we all have faults—no wonder this series of books are more popular in Europe than they are in the United States. We do not like being told we did something wrong, but that does not vaccinate us against a virus of illegitimate ideals of the self.

As we wrap up the involvement of proxies and proctors in Africa leading into World War I and II, we begin to see the spin of proxies against proctors more and more. The Scramble for Africa is documented through history as European nations grab control of resources and resource channels through all parts of Africa. First, let's look at the continent through a very broad and vague lens. Landscape and topography of territories are important to European reasoning and incentive for control and logistical determination to do so. The Sahara expands the vast majority of the northern part of the continent, separating a thin strip of populated land just north between the desert and the Mediterranean. A resource channel can then only be over or under, across and up. Ports exist with access to the Atlantic Ocean to the West and into the Red Sea, Indian Ocean, and access to the Middle East from the eastern part of Africa. Sub-Saharan Africa consists of jungle topography and the majority of resource mines of diamonds, uranium, petroleum, and gold extending all the way to the Southern tip. Ports then exist on each access.

To control trade routes intersecting is then to locate output channels as close to resource locations as possible. The control of southern ports allows direct output control of Gold. East to West allows for majority control of a number of raw material mines, and control of the loop from North to South around the Sahara allows for control of everything. For this, the road race to Fashoda is the clashing point between European nations that leaves its residual effect against natives that begins at the turn of the century and is resolved by the shadowed threat of World War with little to no correlation to friction in Africa.

The enemy of my enemy is my friend, ideology is very simple and applicable even in this scenario. Smaller-scale conflict will always evaporate against the threat of a non-correlated larger conflict. Belgium, Italy, France, Spain, Germany, Britain, and Portugal are at odds. Even as the conflict of Fashoda is cooled, it is not extinguished because, remember, friction and proxy involvement will always leave residuals and the genetic programming of a fire smoldering ready to reignite. As matter is neither created nor destroyed, any European presence is an ember never fully suppressed until complete removal from the equation in both space and time. As World War I is on the brink, and World War II is already timed from 30 years later, a scrabble board is formed, and a game of competitors is to be played.

Viscosity and Velocity

Nothing is constant but change. Our constant is not to say one does not exist, but that one does not remain present as it is before, during, and after manipulation by the universe, whether through an internal or external force. What we do not see in the sciences as they are interpreted today is the change of genetic material in our measurements. We look at the relative placement, speed and effect through causal relationships but not as mass changes rather the position between measurable mass as time and space are manipulated. Our study does not forget this but applies the distinction that not only does relative juxtaposition change but force manipulates the genetic construct of the observed. One does not work without the other. Where relative position applies speed as a measurement of mass in relation to another, we apply viscosity and velocity to measure the rate at which internal manipulation alters the cohesive principles of substance as our genetic coding changes from involved particles.

Symmetry, or supersymmetry, is something we allude to but not something that maintains complete dominance in our study. You cannot say two things in measurement as we are, and show characteristics of symmetrical comparison. Why is this? Because in the change between past, present into the future, our state of constant changing mass with comparative changes in the relative position through space in time will maintain balance over symmetry. At the moment, a measurement of symmetry can be noticed but not one that dominates the entirety of our model. The reason being again, time and space require the tick of a clock to show an effect just as we look into other forms of residual events. You cannot see the complete symmetry of wealth equity the moment $1,400 stimulus checks are sent to millions of people because the process of equity depreciation is felt the moment a transaction is made. A $1400 stimulus check is the analogy of the US Government dropping a penny, discussed in *Volume 2*, but we will only see the residual symmetry through delay when those checks are used to pay for goods, services, or survival resources splintered through space.

Again, symmetry is present, just as the earth's natural laws create new or evolved species of plants or animals, but this process of time delay is only slightly altered. Nutrients always absorb into the seed of a plant without conscious awareness of when that resource should be used. Humanity, however, has a free will variable and accelerant to manipulate time and space and our own genetic mass composition. In our plant analogy, this would be if we decided when and where ourselves as a plant decide to actually absorb rainwater, whether at the right time or the wrong time. Perfect symmetry then does exist in the growth of species of those that are not cognitively aware. The fractal components are not absent within us but again are only available if we want them to be and in which direction our fractal spins and funnels. We can reverse or increase our velocity or viscosity in any general direction at any given point in time.

As defined through a number of sciences, viscosity is the composition and fluidity of a grouping of elements that form a mostly liquid-base. You can measure the viscosity of concrete, but that is not the appropriate use because concrete does not move. You could, though, measure the viscosity of our concrete as we mix our rock mixture and water, and it begins to harden. Slowly in the process, our viscosity rate as our concrete hardens is measured at almost completely 1 in relative terms to only water as 0. High viscosity measures the thickness of a liquid that forces or clogs our fluid dynamic model. Low viscosity is measured as a very malleable material or fluid unhindered by clutter and can move through small spaces without issue or effect upon the model or variables within our vacuum.

Balance within the viscosity rate will always remain. Symmetry will not in the sense that you may think. Symmetry is not if two objects are genetically reciprocal, but rather symmetry is present in the way genetically coded objects are changed. Relativity looks into symmetry as the comparative forces that alter space between and through two or more objects. Symmetry fails in this process because it is not complete, almost as gravitational waves act anomalously or particles collapse due to observation. Symmetry through relativity only measures one-half of the equation to which it will fail. You cannot look into a constant change in time without factoring the constant change of space if you want to find a symmetrical measurement. The math applied to the change in distance needs then to be applied to the change in material composition and computed together as an inverted reciprocal.

Yes, relativity does factor mass and movement as an external influence upon another celestial body. However, as time moves from the past to the present and into the future, we must measure the correlation and conjunction between rapidly changing mass and rapidly changing distance between each mass. A study without this process of thought remains incomplete and viewing the world from only one vantage point. We discovered gravity bends space and time from looking at the sun and moon during a solar eclipse. What we are proposing here then is not that it is incorrect in measuring space-time but that we should then look from the perception of the sun to the moon and then to earth to measure the reciprocal vantage point and see not space-time but time-space. One without the other leaves a study of symmetry always incomplete.

Points on the Board: Cross Up and Across Down

Viscosity is worth 19 points on a board of scrabble without any multipliers or connecting words. Suppose we were to analogize components of a scrabble board. In that case, we think of these invaluable double letters to triple word multipliers in our effort to understand the internal struggle of the state of Africa. Above we summarized the topographic layout of the continent, prioritizing resource sites and channels. We can think of these as multipliers that are consequently useless without connecting and crossing a word to another word. Our crossword connection in itself is just as a resource channel is optimized and present with a low risk of conflict control. Our resources are our multipliers that increase the value of each word that is spelled. Without connecting the first letter to the last letter, our resource and our channel are both useless without the ability to transit across the scrabble board of Africa.

A multiplier is a present dependent on the value associated with that resource. Gold, perhaps, is of higher value than rubber and holds a double word multiplier, while rubber only holds a single letter multiplier. Again, without the completion of the entire word, both are useless, but it is also important to note that once a word is spelled completely, that multiplier as a resource is optimized to one player and cannot be accessed or tapped by another. Though, as it relates to inhabitants of Africa, connecting channels of control, even from another external player, are useful in scoring point value, but our game is optimized when we connect our own channel of words and block the channel spread of another player and block the use of multipliers.

Suppose our board game is laid out and multipliers are placed in geographic locations. In that case, the Sahara is a large section filled with only small multipliers but available if a channel can be made across because more letters and words are focused just south where heavier multipliers are distributed. The goal of one player over the other, or one European nation over another, is to jam their opponent from controlling both raw material resources as well as the channel in which that resource can make it to the outer edge of the board.

At this time period, Britain formulated the word JINGOISM, expanding south to north along the right edge of the board where France had the word EXPANSION from south to north along the left edge. Both countries were missing key letters in the word DOMINANCE crossing and connecting other words along multipliers from West to East. Smaller letters connected with individual letter multipliers, but the issue was the use of another's channel only as a block and not in continuity with their own individual string. Britain also had the word COMMUNICATION expanding parallel from West to East but unconnected from another British string of words. France had a similar scenario from East to West with the word COLONIALISM.

Other European nations such as Belgium and Portugal had much smaller words and control over the board and a lower score through word and letter counts. Multipliers were used but isolated between other larger channels. The process to which this concoction of congestions within our game is then only won by the use and understanding of one winning word to understand our internal prowess creation of internal clogging: VISCOSITY.

Through the mis-optimization of external powers that acted as proctor forces with internal effect, our board became a fluid system toxic of oil-based fluids and other denser components. When water is scarce to begin within, especially in a desert continent, oil or oil-based raw material can clog our system if water is not present to dilute our fluid base. All of a sudden, in our effort for optimization of our fluid vacuum model, it is slowed to the rate molasses or syrup moves relative to the effortless flow of pure hydrogen and oxygen. Our velocity through the vector of space is stagnant but flammable and toxic to the host.

Board Optimization

Viscosity implies the fluid vector can be manipulated based solely on the consistency and genetic makeup of the components moving through a vacuum. The implication is that mass itself, as the occupation of space, is not the only force acting within the vector but also density in fluidity. We use the concept of water moving through a funnel or sands through an hourglass and only see the simple forms of each, but what happens when water turns to oil or that sand is mixed with water or becomes coarse? Each component's genetic density will alter, affect, or erode the model we have formed while moving from one field to the next. An oil-based fluid will leave residual adhesives left in the previous state and slow the process of exchange. Wet sand will likely clog the funnel entirely. Coarse sand will chip away the funnel point if forced through or clog the exchange system in the same way.

Just like the child's toy, a square will never fit through a circular shape with a similar diameter or length across each edge. For this, we should think more into the genetic properties of the countries or entities in play. How can we optimize our scrabble board described above to ensure viscosity does not affect the optimization rate of resource priority for channeling through input to output? The answer is we should not frenzy like a pond of piranhas and scramble for control.

Looking at the figures to follow, think back to our first example of a non-optimized scrabble board across the continent of Africa. Open spaces are left, and the channeling of resources is blocked. What good is a resource for one if the entire channel is closed to the outside world? If the ability to turn raw material into a usable product is absent, that resource is useless even if it carries the weight of the world in gold. Even if that resource channel is open, but with huge expense, that resource still remains useless based on the simplicities in supply and demand and weighing revenue against the expense to remove it. The purpose then is not to leave a board with open spaces but one that pieces together like a Tetris puzzle.

Our Tetris pieces are not simply controlled by one nation or the other, especially if more than one entity is involved. The race to Fashoda became problematic because a fight for control is fought between natives through ideology and false promises from proctor to proxy inhabitants. The channel is simple in a two-dimensional process of exchange, but again, in this day of age, it will never be that simple. A multi-dimensional war or multi-variable complex equation is never solved by simple one-dimensional processes. For this, our Tetris pieces along our Scrabble board are not simply roads but ideologies and applicable governmental controls.

Just as we described in *Volume 2*, a freeway system is present in the effort to understand how we moved input to output succinctly and without roadblocks or bumps. Roads are not paved by only cement but by who, what, where, and why. A roadway is never optimized without the awareness that collective benefit should dominate individual benefit. This, however, is not your single-family farmer that built a road into their field but multinational conglomerates sponsored by country or a powerful individual's pride or scramble for resource control. The residual, as always, when proctors fight for proxy resource control, are the inhabitants that do not have the means to control systems of production or protect their border from invasion.

Just as a tax man hides in the shadows and pops their head out every year around April 15th, the same premise exists. One cannot cooperate with another if a figure in a dark alley lurks. The problem is that both sides see the same thing even if one stands under a streetlight. France and Britain, along with other nations, simply do not understand clear intent and therefore cannot trust the premise that mutually beneficial cooperation can be achieved. I will never trust a dark figure in the shadows of an alleyway because the absence of light does not allow me to see that figure as a non-threat. We cannot naively trust the shadow either without confirmation they do not hold nefarious intent.

Imagine this figure in different shades of Africa as it was pre-World War. A scramble for resource control causes a lapse in optimizing principles. Each channel expresses a resource moving from one sector to another, reaching the edge. Optimization is only allowed to the point in which channels converge, and that resource is prevented from moving freely through time and space. This is a simple form where two entities scramble for control without cooperation. Spaces are left open, and channels are blocked.

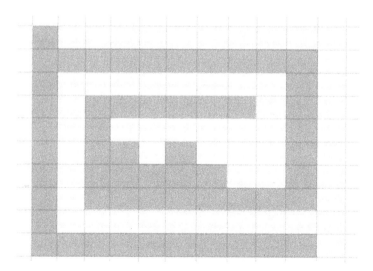

The figure here shows the optimization of two entities that work to channel resources together. Each space on the board is filled while resources are available to be channeled to the outer edge of the board. Cooperation and optimization are then the keys to unlock the relationship as well as transformative resource utilization. At no point do channels block the movement of raw material to the edge of the board. However, this is still not enough. Why? This is in the event raw material is moved away, but what about the inhabitants that own resources by natural law? Optimization is also lost because the channeling of material is not a straight line, as a simple example, to their destination.

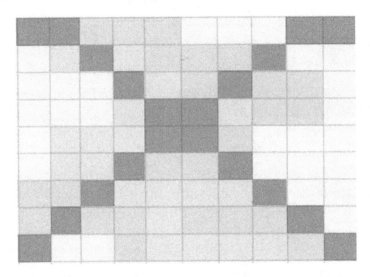

The last figure here shows a multi-variable plot of channels with an independent channel for utilization that crosses each sector of the board that is filled with a separate entity. For each entity, their own channel exists to the point at which most segments can find their way to the edge of the board. The cross-sections, acting as an independent canal, allow for resources of any entity to move diagonally across the board. This independent channel crosses every plot within the board that allows for anyone to access its funnel to output. The question still remains. What about native inhabitants that own rights to raw material moved by proctor nations? They are the owners of this cross-section channel and independent of all proctors. The reasoning is simple. It simply is not right to plunder a nation at the expense of inhabitants and the expense that you may not be aware of toward your own proctor nation.

I could go on and on looking into the hypothetical scenario in which this proxy-controlled channel would be implemented, but that is not our goal at this moment. That is not to say we won't later but at this moment, grabbing the abstract concept and extracting it into your frontal lobe is the only purpose. We are well past barbarism to which pillaging lands for resources should not exist. What does the United Nations do anyways but protect the powerful at the expense of the less fortunate? I know the response is, "We do a lot of good things around the world." Yes, but for you or for them? "We help a lot of people that are in need." Why are they in need? The answer, and substituted solution, is the most complex of them all. How would a proxied nation maintain the rights to their own resources, especially if that nation is at war with themselves or others? How does a nation like Iran or Iraq hold validity when they are deemed a threat to the outside world? Like any other right guaranteed under the constitution, the answer is it is their inalienable right to which we do not have authority to decide. How can one pillage the raw material resources of another under the legitimate or even illegitimate guise of democracy? That, in itself, is not an act of democracy but shadow authoritarianism.

For an act to be allowed, legitimate or not, the question of human nature presents itself in its most consequential terms. The fight for a resource that is not one's own is a decision made by the inhabitants of that territory, whether free or not. For one to arbitrarily decide will always, and shown in history to do so, cause residual toxicity for both proxy and proctor. Any deliberate act to control or constrict the exportation of resources through shadow intent should, with all seriousness, be seen as an act of war and aggression against the peace within our socioeconomic model without authority given and controlled by the host nation with protection of all collected and united nations. The understanding of this concept is vital to the survival of integrity between, within, and among all nations of the world.

Why are migrants fleeing the Middle East? Yes, war has existed for thousands of years, but why now? Not as a direct causal relationship but from the black hole exacerbated by our or another's presence. A black hole is a black hole, but it grows if you give it mass to eat. In reciprocal capacity of resource control, the absence of resources acts to accelerate potential conflict based on the vitality of available material for income where volatility is expected. An act of pillage has an exponential effect when resources are not as readily available for sale and consumption that allow inhabitants to thrive or simply live in peace and harmony. We know this because history tells the story and our principle understanding, even in the continent of Africa, that unavailable resources apply heavier relative weight against those that are present. For a nation rich in oil or natural gas and freshwater, cultivable land, corn, barley, fruits, and vegetables, less weight is propped against an economy that has only one to deal in. Before we are pulled into the whirlpool of proctors and proxies in the Middle East, let's define our third point of reference in the proxy conflict of Africa during the coldest war.

Cold Wars Still Create Heat

During and after World War II, the fight for control of resource channels approaches a tipping point as new useful materials are found. Uranium mines throughout the continent are now increasing in value during an arms race and the proliferation of nuclear weapons. Treaties signed after World War II place new regulations upon how a foreign nation can involve themselves in another foreign land as a definable act of aggression. However it's simple, the nation of the Congo isn't too worried about a treaty between Russia and the United States when personal survival is more real and an immediate concern, even if the involvement with either superpower kicks the can of mutual destruction only a bit further down the road.

The cost of World War II left Britain, France, and other nations scrambling to reestablish the homeland after Germany's destructive blitzkrieg and bombardment. Uranium, not only oil, gold, and rubber, is accessible to once partial allies and now shadow enemies. The use of proxies reaches its peak spin rate, but why then is this called a Cold War when all wars create friction? It is not cold to the inhabitants fighting as proxies for each nation where the polarity of friction is injected by proctor versus proctor and into each proxy. Friction is present but not directly against or felt by enemies at odds. Blood is only spilled by spies of each, but more blood is spilled by armies they control fighting under a different flag and different cause. What we see in this instance is the complete transformation from one to two to the third dimension of conflict. Where our rate of involvement began as a simple one or two-dimensional circle in a vector of space, a perfect spinning sphere is the new reality. The reason this makes sense, as mass changes into new forms, new characteristics are present. One against the other, in duality, is simply one dot on a line against another. Just as in the Wild West, a duel solved the dispute between one person that just doesn't like the other. Add millions of other people and hundreds of thousands of soldiers fighting for a cause they are not directly aligned with but act parallel to, and we create new dimensions of conflict and friction.

Speed, force, and energy are never lost. If one entity acts against another by indirect measures, that does not mean a war remains cold. If energy is added in conflict through indirect acts of aggression, our accelerant, through ideology or resource control, creates spin, not movement through space. Spinning fast enough, beyond the ability of our vehicle to maintain homeostasis; the wheels fall off. The irony, spinning fast enough and colliding is almost like the complexities of atoms or hydrogen bombs crashing particles together or splitting them. It only depends on which perspective we look into this scenario from. From the perspective of humanity as a whole, the action of two entities against another splits the entirety of humanity apart into a burning ember. From the perspective of each super-entity, the act is more through the reaction of fusion energy and force of one atom into another without regard for human life. What happens in both scenarios? Mutually assured destruction. Proxy conflict deeper into the Cold War is then becoming a Super Bumper of two proctor nations but a trojan virus from the perspective of inhabited proxied nations.

The Congo Crisis

For at least one historical representation of this form of proxy conflict during the Cold War, we look into the Congo Crisis in the early 1960s. Newly declared independent from previous governance, new authority in place faced constant acts of insurrection. The grasp of control and threat of not only revolt but death is that immediate danger we speak of. Without the assistance of the United States in fighting against revolt and sectarian violence, the Congolese government turned to the Soviets. Sustenance of life in volatility is time sensitive data to which the shrinking of space between can only be separated by a timely protector. A worrying thought for Americans because this meant control of rich uranium mines that held high-quality material even used against the Japanese at Hiroshima was lost to the Soviets. Coup after coup led to proxy conflict at the hands of proctors. Inhabitants, a semi-established government, and insurrectionists are at odds and spun into a war for control accelerated by the spin rate of mixed ideological purpose and intent over resources. For the US and the Soviet Union, the resource of uranium is the accelerant. For both sides on the ground, life and authority control is the accelerant mixed in both ideology and resource potency. What do proctors do? Manipulate space and time to bend reality.

Weaponry and other forms of support stir conflict into a full proxy war. The hot war is fought with rifles, where the cold war is fought with the threat of a very, very hot war. Manipulate physical force and add the thought of big brother support, and you control the territory in which resource control can be won or lost by either side. As the Soviet Union and United States flood armies with cold deposits of cold hard cash and unfired rockets and bullets, risk heats up. The bureaucracy in conflict is apparent. Sure, one soldier killing another ends the life for one and gains a territorial advantage for another, but this is not where the duel ends. As one Congolese soldier moves against an insurgent, it is like one Soviet soldier-spy moving against an American soldier-spy. A battle of intellect is fought through the movement of physical chess pieces and very real soldiers fighting an ideology war through the interpretation of authority resource control. The movement through ideology conflict holds a subsequent movement in resource conflict. Previous wars throughout even the dark ages, with sticks and stones, are fought head-to-head in dualistic and dynamic conflict. The presence of technological advancements of weaponry, communication abilities, and aptness to move quickly through space and on land or in the air allows for this to occur. We are now fighting wars through the dimensions. Looking into the figures previously, we can summarize the way in which war in Africa has evolved in less than one hundred years to spin at a rate to which control is impractical, improbable, and impossible.

Proxy conflict in Africa is easy to justify through the eyes of superpower diplomatic representatives until space and time are reduced to frictional capacity. Proxy conflict during the Cold War creates controllable fire in Africa as it relates to the Soviet or United States mainland. What happens, though, when spin is rapidly increasing to the point of instability, and then you close the gap in space and time? You have the Cuban Missile Crisis where the spin of time creates uncontrollable energy when the space between two involved entities is reduced. Conflict spins frictional heat only cooled through expansion and space between particles. That is how evaporation works. Steam is heat subdued by spreading particles of hydrogen and oxygen apart. What happens when you encapsulate that steam into a jar and crank up the hurt? Glass shards fly every which way with no regard for human life. Spin those particles out of control and then plant missiles close in space to an involved entity; disaster is a fusion reaction away.

Proxy Conflict in the Middle East: The Whirlpool Effect

What causes water to boil and evaporate? Heat. What happens when an ocean is superheated, and hydrogen and oxygen cannot bond? The only thing left is the ocean floor; sand. Granted, the Middle East at one point in the evolution of the Earth was not all underwater, or perhaps I don't know, but the point remains applicable. Whether or not a plethora of water existed within the Middle East territories is irrelevant when we know what remains, nothing in the sands of time. Just as conflict exists in the continent of Africa and spills back and forth into Iran and Iraq and all other nations bordering one another, excessive heat does everything from not allowing plants to be cultivated through unfruitful soil to simply making people angry and uncomfortable.

On a hot summer day, without proper ways to cool the human body, life simply sucks. Granted, we get a few days out of the year that peak over 100 degrees, but not like the summers where conflict seems to be second nature. Sure, North Korea, Russia, and China all have climates that do not cause the same environmental heat wave scenario and still have internal conflicts, but the environment, through a nurturing process as a dominant variable, can have enough of an effect to completely dissolve all reason and logic or even nature's pure intent. Starvation and dehydration do crazy things to the human mind willing to do anything to survive and maintain individual ability to thrive just a little more than another, even if a negative effect is felt for a neighbor and the overall collective. Human nature to survive, in life-threatening scenarios, will always be dominant if nurture does not allow sustenance. We naturally need water the Earth can nurture us with. If we are not

119

nurtured in this way, nature's intent for survival by any means exists as an individual drives against the common collective goal.

It is tough to think of the needs of another if all we can think about is an unquenchable and insatiable thirst. Just as when we are hungry, our low level needs must be met before we can realize the effort of actualization of one in a collective of all. When one can sate their insatiable thirst, it is much easier to quell the same thirst in another if the resource is available. In the Middle East, since the dawn of time, as it seems, this is not something that has been possible. If you then take from a well that is almost dry, the negative effect on all others is felt exponentially. The burning of the sun takes its toll on even the most naturally gifted creatures. It is hard to be happy when you can feel your skin burn. Happiness is not even a realistic goal. And for this, governance is based on the survival of one as opposed to the thriving of all.

Spinning Sand When Water is Required

In *Volume 2*, we discussed the fuller thought behind a field state vacuum and fluid dynamics associated with pulling trickle-down economics into the socio by adding a number of new variables. Everything that goes into an input to output system is applied for the effort of seeing the full picture. The simplicity in a two-dimensional approach does not solve a problem in the third and only creates a differentiation in the end product. For us here, this is seen in the historical evidence and application of two-way logic where the trinity of dynamic properties is apparent and even more relevant. As opposed to a two-way street, we see this street in terms of the vehicles on the road and their relative juxtaposition to each other.

Just as an automobile requires clean gas and oil, our vehicle, in terms of a socioeconomic model in a fluid state, requires a pure water source. Just as a car that is filled with water instead of gas breaks down, our system can become non-functional in the event sand is added and the relative measurement of any other deposit removes from a zero point pure state of hydrogen and oxygen. The rate at which sand is added and water removed is the way in which our system's engine is stalled. Even if sand is added and even more water is added to dilute our concoction, the mixture's potency as an accelerant can fight against the system it turns. The reason being, there is only so much space in a gas tank. You can throw one bucket of sand back into the ocean, and it will sink to the bottom and almost instantly be a non-solvent in a bucket's measure of ocean water.

This is, again, very fundamental to our principles in that we are not trying to encapsulate the ocean, but measure an open system based upon the dynamics of closed system theories and applications. We do not measure the value of resources against a meteor in outer space that holds the same raw material, but we are valuing resources based on a ratio spectrum in relative terms as percentiles of resources that are available. In a moment in time, that meteor filled with diamonds could crash into the Earth with no negative physical impact upon life but completely tip the scale of relative value in the diamond industry.

At any given point in time and space, any measurement can change by an externally or internally influential event such as a meteor or a constant civil war over control channels of input to output in both ideology and material value to the inhabitants in close proximity of space or time. For us, going back to our thoughts of Iran, Iraq, Syria, Israel, Jordan, Turkey, Afghanistan, and so on, we must look into the field state of affairs in this light. Our gas tank lacks a pure water source and is constantly filled with a large supply of sand where there is just enough water to sustain life but not allow life to thrive.

In a desert, sand is abundant, and the unfortunate irony is present and abundant as well. Nothing is worse than taking a drink of water and gulping a heap of sand. Biologically, we consume enough of it, and we can die. Dark and tragic but just that simple. The resource readily available to boost economic prowess in the Middle East is a topic of concern for many other proctor nations and is seen throughout news and governance topics from nations all over the world. Do I need to even say it? Obviously, oil. The transformative property for inhabitants in the Middle East is not to power their vehicles or power plants but to transform that oil into water. I do not mean that in the physical and chemical property of doing so, but oil is turned into dollars. Dollars are turned into anything you want. Water, medication, food, but the unfortunate reality is then the power to provide those necessities in exchange as well. One can be manipulated to act in such a way if you hang a carrot of survival in front of them and quell their thirst every once in a while to which the inevitability of that same thirst to return is guaranteed and then manipulated against again.

The Persian Gulf is filled with blood, toil, oil, and tears expended for dollar-to-dollar value, where multinational efforts to mitigate the effects of conflict are to sustain the channel of a resource. The difference between the Middle East and other internal conflicts involving proctor and proxy is that physical force is the cause instead of the effect. In the causal relationship, physical force and conflict are present by ideology first instead of resource control first. Looking at previous chapters, we see that the continent of Africa is a scrabble board based on controlling a resource to which violence followed. In the Middle East, this relationship is inverse and measured almost into the beginning of time. This is the difference between a Black Hole and a supermassive Black Hole. Nature is affected by nurture. In Africa, nurture is affected by nature.

The hope for the continent of Africa is slightly brighter than the Middle East for this reason. Proxy conflict through proctors spin the logic of reality in war to the furthest edge of the universe and consume anything in its path. The balance of collective nature versus nurture then dictates the gravitational force as two or more entities become involved within the space and time our base liquid exists as well as the viscosity measurement of genetic components. For some nations about to be invaded by a proctor, a ticking time bomb only waits with the most catastrophic consequences if a match is lit. If one is to fight a war after a terrorist attack based on ideology, one cannot remain only for resources without establishing a self-sufficient entity in its place when the proctor is removed. If we don't do so, we are Perseus fighting the Kraken but also feeding and training it as well.

The Whirlpool: Proctors of Proxies

The mythological analogy of Perseus and the Kraken is not what you may think it to be. This does not mean we are arming and training the Taliban, even if we are, but that we are feeding the Kraken as we remain with the intent of removing ourselves without establishing infrastructure allowed for self-sustenance. This is the vacuum you read in the papers forcing migrants to flee ISIS and other terrorist organizations. A whirlpool that does not discriminate.

As proctors spin proxies sooner or later, the laws that dictate the relationship between nature and nurture reach a boiling point and invert dominant capabilities and capacities. Natural tendency to grow by nurturing characteristics inverts to which nurturing traits grow through natural tendency. Even as a Volcano erupts in the Bahamas and destroys living things, plants, and coral reefs, life continues to grow after molten rock cools and ash clouds dissipate. However, imagine that same Volcano erupts, and nothing returns. No regrowth. No Darwinist will to survive and evolve. Nothing. Sand replaces any water source available, and our thirst for water remains, but we consume sand thinking the insatiable will be sated. Our logic and reason skew in a way that sand tastes like water but does not genetically convert to energy or sustain life within. This is our involvement with ISIS, Iran, and Iraq in the Middle East. Anything left in the shadows will always come into the light.

The year is 1908, and the first oil drill finds a valuable resource in Iran. 1913, Britain knocked on the door. Iranian discontent with royalty-share soon followed. The year is 1938, the largest oil well on Earth is found in Saudi Arabia. The year is 1941, Britain and the USSR invade Iran and establish proctor dominance. Nationalism in Iran soon followed, and external proctors were met with ideological confrontation.

Coup after coup met 1954 with a political agenda between outside nations to reestablish control. Saudi Arabia met the United States upon frictional agreement levied and hedged by mutually beneficial terms. Non-agreement would have likely resulted in conflict. The 1973 Arab-Israeli war soon followed as Israel's ideological tension with Arab nations reached a peak affecting a separate accelerant resource. Just as viscosity is either wet sand or dry sand, the teetering is between the two. A balance in ideology and resource control centered around cohesive principles of collected involvement, absence of adhesive ideology removes sand from the equation completely. You could analogize a measurement of oil or blood into our fluid genetic makeup to add other variables, but for simplicity's sake, sand is enough. However, each grain acts in its own potency as each grain of sand on earth is different from another. For this, we have mites that create moles to dig holes.

Infestation: Infinitesi-mites, Infinitesi-moles, and Holes

Mites are bugs that feed on a number of things. Moles are critters that burrow. Holes are just holes in the ground. Add infinity to the equation, and we begin digging holes into the space-time vector of a vacuum and leak controlled pressure and dynamic control of internal substances. The oddity is the name of a Black Hole is that the term does not accurately depict what exactly it is. A hole is a hole limited in its form. A Black Hole is an infinitely deep point in space leading into a measurement of singularity. The illusion is there is a bottom, but that is not how singularities work but only how holes work. A hole in space digs itself. A hole in the ground requires a shovel or something or someone to dig it. That is where I beg to differ against the thought applied to the definition of a Black Hole. The application of these three components, mites, moles, and holes, can then be applied to the functions of society that create catastrophic collapse with whirling quagmire traits. Sure, whatever, I am wrong in the next sentence by all definable characteristics in that mites do not make moles. Ok, noted. Moles have their own traits. I just like mites and moles, and I will at least let it make sense until someone comes along and re-defines it. That's fine.

A mite is a polar charged particle that groups together to make a mole. A mole, by the law of averages, will have one definable polar charge, to which they then dig into the vector of our model. Just like a vacuum that cleans dirt up off your floor, a mole punches a hole as if you vacuumed up a nail to which a hole is formed. At this point, our vacuum loses pressure. For a socioeconomic application, mites are all the little parts within the space in play and add up through averaging all into one variable then an effect caused by our mole. By this, our hole is formed.

Just like when a star goes into supernova, molecular, chemical, and genetic characteristics dictate the power of our mole and hole into the fabric of space. Infinitesi-mites then are all those little minute particles. If we are to measure these against society, we should remember our process applies mass that constantly changes with each tick of the clock. At one point in time, a person through an event in history has the choice to enact a positive or negative charge. If a member of ISIS removes evil intent, they have changed their genetic composition for that moment in time. Just as a fluid dynamic state, the trend of all manipulates other mites and the mole as a whole and sum of all.

Infinitesi-mites then are the very small components of the measured field state. Are inhabitants of this field state ideologically cohesive with outside forces or with reality in general? Is the polar charge of each mite an attracting or repelling charge to the involved entities, and at what level of charge? All these things matter and more. Is the governing body of the proxy nation cohesive with the proctor? Not usually ever the case but some relatively more than others. A nation that wants democracy against barbarism will align and converge until accelerants diverge through purpose and intent. With the known fact that energy is neither created nor destroyed, only misplaced, looking past one evil for a lesser evil continues to tick a time bomb just by kicking it down the road; friction temporarily mitigated.

Iraq and Iran in the Iranian revolution in the 1970s act as forces against one another, and the United States's involvement in the shadows is seen just enough in dim light. By the late 1980s and 1990s, when the Gulf War was in full swing, the purpose became evident. Are we aggressive for ideological differences or for resource control, or for one to excuse and rectify the other? You can then continue to think of infinitesimites as insurgent soldiers on the ground. You can think of the type of commodity trade as a mite as well. You can think of any member within a mosque or church, any community neighborhood, any family, any school, any leader, any proctor soldier, any measure of resource or ideology, or anyone or thing within the state involved.

Jumping to September 11, 2001, a mole punched a hole to which we responded. However, in the name of democracy, limited available resources in the sands of the Middle East did not allow for sustainability upon departure. It is hard to fuel an army only on oil when they struggle for water or to escape the heat. You cannot hydrate a population without a lake or resource to allow for them to drink. This is a simplification of the problem but in the complexity of its understanding, useful. If a vacuum exists where the walls and fabric holding it together is one resource, it is quite easy for a nail to puncture a hose bleeding pressure and losing containment. Take oil from China; they will be fine, aggressive, but fine. Destroying infrastructure that already is only 1% of what is needed for democracy to exist, your goal is futile and unfruitful, just as the ground that lacks nutrients you wish to cultivate agricultural resources upon.

As time goes on and war continues, and the Taliban is drawn out, and the combatants that brought down megastructures in the US are neutralized, the cause of staying will show its effect upon leaving. The US begins withdrawing troops, and infinitesimites lose their polar opposite charge and support instability to the field that remains. Just as the US acts only to clog a hole in our vacuum's hose, we are enlarging it as each rocket is fired and bomb dropped. The hole is wider, widening and then what happens upon removal?

What happens next is important to understand as space to which our center of conflict grows into Europe and the US through the use of time beyond space to reach us at home. Attacks in Paris, throughout the UK, Germany, Belgium, and the US, take place. Perhaps not at the scale of September 11th, but the effect is still the same. We feel unsafe now, even in the space of our own homes based on something that occurred thousands of miles away. Just as a hair, hypothesized, from a hole can reach out like a tentacle and manipulate gravity just enough for one person or particle to escape and affect the reality of another.

This may seem complex in understanding and not as simple as it should be because that is the reality. This is the most complex diplomatic issue in the entire world. Here are some images and figures to help our understanding.

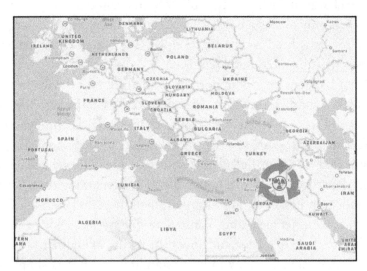

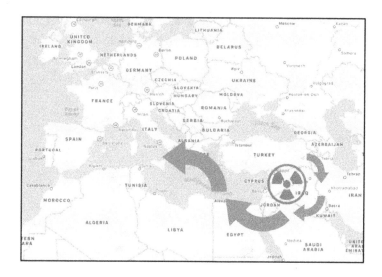

As war begins, insurgency is suppressed but not expelled unless our job is complete. Sure, the United States of America's goal is to not remain in the Middle East for thousands of years, but that was the solution when we knocked on the door. If democracy and freedom were the operations in play, the equation was simple, but the time it would take innumerable. The effect was clear as well. The vacuum that would ensue after removing ourselves from the equation is what we received and nothing more or less. Sure, things had cooled a bit since then but not to the point at which our effort was intended when we began. Democracy was the idea. Control was the intent. Control of what? Ideology? Or resources?

Sure, our purpose in Iraq and Iran has been mitigated since the highest peak threat of ISIS and the height of the Taliban, but the risk lurks in the shadows. Why was it mitigated? Resource demand is low, and the supply is high with other tapped sources and renegotiations with Saudi Arabia and other exporters around the world. About a year ago now, the price of oil reached the lowest point in my short history, where the cost to store oil was higher than the cost to throw it away. I have never seen a barrel of oil reach a negative price index. Surprisingly enough, conflict is low in relative terms to years in the past. I probably could say these two thoughts are not directly correlated, but they are surely not non-variable against the acceleration to or from armed conflict. You can also very simplistically without complete direct correlation say a pandemic that reduced the use of oil and gas quelled and displaced frictional energy and tension between proxy and proctor nations in the Middle East. Energy displaced but not removed.

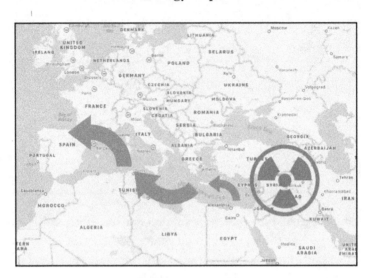

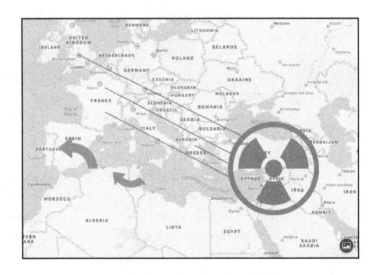

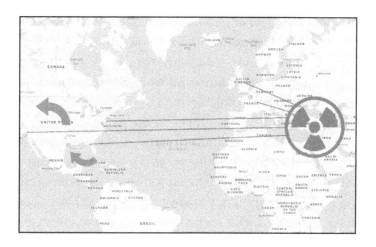

Hairs and Scares Create Scars

Before Stephen Hawking passed away, he likely proved the non-existence of hairs extending from a Black Hole or at the very least information consumed from a Black Hole would escape through Hawking radiation or be stretched and consumed into singularity until the Black Hole died. The thing here is I am not going to say this to be true or false because the point of observation to prove this true or not is intransigent, untransmittable, and unable to be transited. Plus, I have not put in the same time in observing the mathematics of Black Holes as Hawking. Meaning, you have to sit in a Black Hole and look outward to see if there is information that can escape because, from our perspective, we only see what is consumed. The inverse reality present, however, would then allow you to hypothesize what you would see if you sat inside one. Because this point in the space of infinite density still exists in our three-dimensional universe, I would only imagine what you would see as you sit beyond the horizon. You would see everything we see looking into new images of Black Holes but upside down and backward where things are quirky and bent. As you look from the inside, you would see not what is consumed but what is created and expelled. What do I think about this and why? My reasoning holds a very weird answer. Eyes.

As we then look deeper into our topic of hairs and scares and the Middle East, we should look into the diagrams formed. Once the United States and other forces move out of the proxied region, the strength of unstable negatively charged infinitesimites increases, and friction creates energy requiring space to cool, forcing our vector to grow, reach and stretch. As refugees and infinitesimites escape across the Mediterranean and the border to Turkey and into Europe, a few negatively charged particles make it through. For this, we see the atrocities against civilian people simply living their lives. I do not want to name these attacks, but I am sure, if you were present, you are aware of what I am alluding to. The darkness associated with such violence is not one I wish to dissect in that way. The sanctity of life and peace is then scarred, only repaired and re-skinned in time with healing.

The Earth and accompanied world that lives here is a genuinely and genetically good place, but pockets of evil do exist. What we are saying is not that the US or any other European nation acted with ill intent, but when you knock on a neighbor's door, you must prepare yourself for what you may not see behind that door upon approach. Unfortunately, not everyone can be saved even if our goal is pure because our effort to do so transforms our own intent as we become involved in a quagmire of ill-willed fate. The inevitability is present, and the effect can grow a pocket of misfortune beyond all pockets of fortune. We are fortunate to live in a democratic nation, and those that live under a similar system of governance should recognize this fortune without the force of perfection that is unattainable. To pretend the government can supply every need and every want you have is absurd. Sometimes life just sucks. That is life. Sometimes life is amazing. That is just life. The ebbs and flows will remain, and we must do our best to be aware of this fact and not let any high or low negatively affect our own experience here as well as someone else for our own negation. The understanding of this allows us to encapsulate the uncontrollability of an open system.

Trojan Substance and Replicative Processes

To revert back to our biological analysis as we venture more into the macro-celestial understanding of events, we should look into our hairs and scars as trojan substances. Because we allude and metaphorically apply the micro to the macro, we should link our hairs just as a trojan substance would invade the body of a cell as a virus. Just as universe sets and states or nations become involved, particles are shared in the form of ideological thought of and between. Most people have a conceptual idea of those in Iraq. Most people that have a conceptual idea are likely misconceiving that thought into misconception. The shadows on the cave wall either make them our enemy or our friend. How many people that hate someone from Iraq or Iran do you think have ever met someone that lived there? Probably no one. Anyone that decides to be emotionally attached to the conception they form likely are more non-objective. Meaning, they probably didn't even know and found out after they had a friendly conversation. Why? Because we are all just people subject to certain inflamed biases misconstrued by our own self-fulfilling logic.

I actually have met a few people from Iran, Iraq, Israel, Palestine, and other nations and have found their culture to be intriguing. In one of my classes at Sacramento State University, I had the pleasure of meeting someone from Israel, to which I will never forget the experience they shared. It amazes me, as I am sure it amazes them, the tragedy of comfort of the American population. Do you think your phone dying sucks? Imagine being in a restaurant minding your own business, and a bomb goes off right outside or hearing machine gunfire daily. Imagine that happening just as often as your phone dies, or as you drink your

133

morning coffee, because you obsess about keeping it charged. This is the real world, not a fallacy.

A Trojan substance is then the ideology mutated through the eyes of hate. Most people form opinions reciprocally as well. Yes, we in the United States are uncomfortable with our phone battery dying to which the perspective observed by the other side can become hateful as well. This is not a product of collective culture but an individual's natural inability to process the nurturing effect of life and emotion in general caused by both experiences and genetics. People that do harm to others most often have harm done to them previously, but the process in which we transmute these events shapes the psyche. A trojan can then be internal as well as external.

Domestic terrorism or insurgent terrorism is the difference in how hate is manipulated into an action. A domestic terrorist forms a thought about their home from another member of their home. An insurgent terrorist forms a thought about their neighbor from a member of their home. The third form is then a domestic insurgent terrorist, which manipulates the mind to form a thought about a member of their home from their neighbor. If we were to equate these to historical events, it is quite simple. Timothy McVay, the Oklahoma City bomber, and the KKK are domestic terrorists. The hijackers on September 11th are insurgent terrorists. The third and most insidious form is how time manipulates our idea of space. Through the internet, insurgents manipulate vulnerable members of the home to act in aggression against their home. Each form is a trojan, and the definition is how they enter the cell's body externally as a virus or from within as a malignant cancer or as an outside agent entering and then forming malignancy.

A domestic terrorist is a malignant cell that grows on information they consume and becomes cancerous as nicotine can invade the receptors of the lungs. An insurgent terrorist would almost be second-hand smoke causing malignancy to grow. A domestic insurgent would then almost be the same consumption of nicotine, but instead of lung cancer, they get brain cancer. Each one slowly kills the host. In a different context, as we talk about disease and trojans, obviously, the most popular topic right now is a virus.

The way a virus moves is incredibly smart as they are not yet alive until they attach to a host. Just as an idea cannot be founded in reality or acted upon until it is accepted or validated, stupidity is a virus just as much as COVID-19 is. The way in which a virus moves is important in our logic. Previously we discussed how conflict could arise similar to the pairing and bonding of chemical components within the transcription and translation of DNA and RNA. Just the same as a virus can manipulate our genetic biological process, so can it to our psychological biology. Sure, serotonin and dopamine are not what we are looking at in this volume but maybe. Rather, we are looking analogously to how a virus of thought can cause mass-replication of who we are, and act based solely in the moment of a thought as a virus as opposed to a healthy thought from within.

A virus is not living until it attaches to a living cell and replicates. If we are to diagnose our style of trojan influence, it is just the same. A virus is formed in the space of accelerant manipulation and creation to which it enters a new host and becomes alive. The question is, is our accelerant made at home or at our neighbors, and does it move mass because of us, or do we act because we consumed the thought from the source. If we were to become patient zero and infected, do we infect our family as well? Do our family members have up to date virus protection? Meaning, a group of Klansmen can breathe ideology where the virus can move hosts and replicate within those that align. Or, do we knowingly have a virus living within and go to our neighbor's house unmasked and expose them as well, to which they act out against their home? Or, does our neighbor become infected and act with aggression against us directly? The first scenario is domestic terrorism. The second is domestic insurgent terrorism. And the third is insurgent terrorism. To help us visualize this, let's look at the image below.

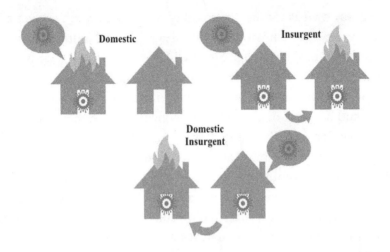

In the same way, a number of different bacteria or viruses can enter the cell body, or a cancerous malignancy can grow from genetic misfortune; the transmission process is analogous to the way in which pockets of intent can infiltrate the home or act in perspective to our neighbor. If the least we have to do is wear a mask, that is not too much to ask if you ask me. Whether one believes a grand conspiracy, to dive into those depths is something I do not have time to think about, nor should I, for it does not get you anywhere but into fantasy. I am more worried about the process in which you or another have come to the realization of that fantasy and the vulnerability and gullibility that you should also be aware and afraid of.

To fight the "grand scheme" against you is not to dive into those depths but defend yourself against the gaps in logic and reason within you, not another. Just as a domestic, insurgent, or domestic insurgent terrorist, vulnerability is culpability if an action is taken against your neighbor. Just as one must ensure their process is sound, one must encapsulate their own field vector and defend against the virus of trojan thoughts. Normally, they are not your own, but they replicate as if they are and justify themselves and yourself against the faulty logic found by another infected host. The process is the same as we read of shadow terror cells or domestic terror groups or webpages grabbing the vulnerable and showing them how to make pressure cooker bombs. Boston. Paris. Sweden. Las Vegas. New York. Florida. Belgium. Nice. Tragedies that are unacceptable.

True/False Victim Theory

Just as the virus of thought described above, the way in which we perceive an event forcing one into the antagonist role can be correlated to how we view ourselves as a victim of nature or nurture. When someone is on trial for a crime, a victim is presumed to be part of the case. The guilt or innocence of the perpetrator is determinant of the court's ability to explain the event that caused the victimization of another. If we were to invert this approach in theoretics, guilt or innocence is then dependent on the true/false equation and weight of perpetration upon the victim. I am not saying we should presume innocence or guilt of the perpetrator in this way, only that we can visualize a crime from both points of view. In this, we can justify the correlation of an event to decipher intent and effect upon the victim in logic and rationality.

More often than not, the victimization of one is due to the perpetrators' perceptive response to true or false victimization in past experience. Sure, one can be abused as a child and grown in a negatively nurturing environment. That still does not justify a crime. What we are looking into is whether or not the perception of the perpetrator is shaped in falsehood. Just the same as the discomfort of a cell phone dying relative to bomb explosions as a part of life can measure the way in which victimization occurs and is felt by the perceiver. True or falsehood in this philosophical equation is dependent on either nature or nurture. If victimization aligns with falsehood, it is much more likely that the emotion died with a natural response. If it aligns with the residual of nurture in life, a true measurement would be noted in rationality, which is tough to decipher. The figure below helps us understand this idea further. I would also like to note this theory likely exists, but I have not read anything about it, so I wish to clarify this may or may not be thought of as my own but shared similarly aligned with the thoughts of another in official and intellectual property and capacity. Whatever.

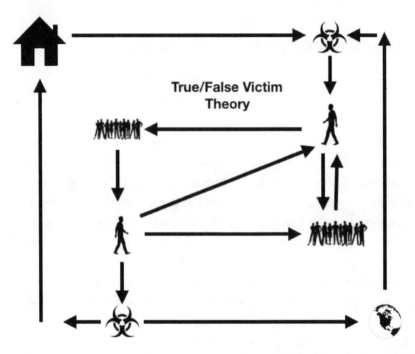

Just as a whirlpool exists sweeping and consuming all things involved in the proximity of space and time, so does the cascading reality of what makes someone a victim and then a perpetrator. Most people, if victimized, do not abhorrently act against another. However, it is likely the victim, in this case, will shape a demographic characterization of someone they see as a threat. An abused child, alcohol, and a drunken father may look and feel unsafe when in the proximity of a bar or someone that shows similar traits. Someone that has experienced racial degradation may look at the perpetrator and make an assumption of the collective that maintains the same visual characteristics just as an explosion that rocks a cafe or post-traumatic stress disorder of veterans of war makes the sound of a car backfiring a programmed event or characterization that causes a fearful response of fight or flight.

To look into the figure above, I want you to think of just what we have described in the previous subchapter in how one virus of thought infects another and enacts a response against the home or their neighbor.

Through nurture and toxicity, it can be determined the way in which a vulnerable host can be infected by a pathogen, whether deliberate or by chance. One that naturally has the emotion of hate will cling to and enjoy the power of radioactive thought justification they feel when another validates their own personal anger. The encouragement to maintain independence from their neighbor and isolate in a home of thought allows a virus to infect and manipulate. This remains a determinant to both the home and the individual, and only leaves remains absent of the spirit of humanity.

Racism in the United States is a product of this process of thought, but so is the rebuttal that all majorities are racist against the demographic of one as a whole. The generalization places fear through both pairs of eyes and makes it as if both are creatures lurking in the shadows. I know, with current historical events and ones preceding in historical context, that I naturally tread lightly in certain scenarios in fear of misinterpretation from biased and skewed emotion in reasoning inflamed by contextual thought present in society. The friction between two points of view is accelerated into conflict, and embers fanned into ignition solely on the broad characterization of one defined as the sum of all.

The toxicity of an event, depicted in the figure, spins the reasoning of one to manipulate what is seen and interpreted of the world around and their neighbors. From previous events affecting one individual, a group can feel the side-effect unbeknownst to a cascading tragedy in reason. Isolation from interpreting the intent of another is at fault. Awareness is the bridge that brings us back together.

Individual two feels the effect of individual one and takes it home with them. Individual two wakes up and walks the world viewing group one based on the initial event of toxicity. Individual one aligns with the personal demographics of group one, creating friction between individual one and individual two and group two. The view of the world and mixture of this friction within the home looking back out into the world and against the demographically associated group of another writes conflict into reality. How then do we diagnose true or falsehood? Individual two will always maintain victimization. Individual one is a victim of nurtured events that cycle between their position as individual one or two.

As the arrows rotate around the grid, one and two change position creating a cause or effect in differing perspective scenarios. Toxicity is measured by this transfer around the map of reason. The determination of true or falsehood is which individual is which. By this map, neither individual one nor individual two are specified as we explained; they constantly change position. As the arrows cross in the center, the generalization and assumption of an individual aligned with a group, and the same inverted process, shows true or false victimization.

A white supremacist creates a victim as the natural solidification of ignorance through falsely nurtured justification. A minority as a victim of the same white supremacist maintains true victim status. This does not remove that same minority as the perpetrator in a future event, but the number of contextual acts against them in degradation shapes a predictable response of natural response to survive as opposed to maintaining dominance. A majority individual that aligns with perceptual demographics can be murdered during a riot and still hold true victim status in this event to which the minority individual exposed to true victimization in past events places falsehood against their perpetration, acting out as a victim of the previous subjectification. This is not to say an act is right or wrong but apply the understanding of both the perpetrator as the cause and conceptualize the interpretation of effect against a victim as a residual moving through society just as a virus of ill-will and intent is spread. Viruses, unlike people, do not know prejudice or injustice or even racism. They understand infection.

Through the Pupil

If you think good things, good things happen. If you think bad things, bad things happen. If you think good thoughts, you can act on good thoughts. If you think bad thoughts, you act on bad thoughts. If you think good thoughts, good acts cause others to think good thoughts. If you think bad thoughts, bad acts cause others to think bad thoughts. If you think bad thoughts and act on bad thoughts, causing others to think bad thoughts, they act on bad thoughts. A bit of a quandary to think about but let us act on it: through the eye, no light can escape. It's dependent on the viscosity of what is observed and how the interpreter naturally siphons and rationalizes logic from an event of nurturement.

People always say you perceive reality as a consumer but also can create reality as a producer. It may not be as others imagine it, but it is true to a certain degree as we think about the acts of nature and nurture. It is not that you simply think about $10 million and it falls from the sky, but thinking positive thoughts about your work increases its value. Thinking bad about the work you create can only then decrease its value. The product of nature to act as a nurturing variable is to say that you can only add positivity into an unbiased experience. Each experience through the perceiver can be worse or better than the relative perception of another. We used the example of a cell phone dying and car bombs exploding. Nature presents the event as a part of life. In our experiences it only becomes natural to weigh positivity or negativity against another event to follow. For one to experience car bombs constantly, you would think a phone dying is peanuts. For one to experience a phone dying and never feel the heat of an explosion, reality is comforted through non-extreme stressed events to where we can naturally create tension upon minuscule discomforts relative to macro discomfort. What we mean here is, in a balanced system, or person, measurement within the spectrum of extremes can create, by nurtured experience, our likelihood to perceive an event predictably within that spectrum.

Sure, you have other synchronic events where it seems you indeed think a thought, you see, but we won't dive that deep. Let's just say more than once while typing these excerpts with the television on or music playing that I have typed an odd and elaborate word or phrase and have heard at the exact moment each letter is entered. *Vision* and *neighbor* are words I recall as an optometry commercial switched on or channel two news reported, and I typed the same word phrases in each moment. *Balance* is another. So is the word *bridge* as I wrote the introduction to this volume but predetermined the title months ago. The term *right and wrong was typed* later in this book on April 18th at 7:13 am while listening to channel four local bay area news as they spoke of harassment against Asian minorities in the Bay Area. The word *Resolute* further into this document during a Warriors game broadcast. At this point, I notice them but move right along and log them in the past. The idea that we manifest the life we want and directly the experiences we have is almost witchcraft to those that do not see or create the world in front of them but grasp and hope for the best without controlling personal internal response against an event that leads to a choice. Emotion dominates logic. Wonder is never a bad thing. Complete restraint against thought is. A thought is never anything to be fearful of until you are unable to control your actions against the process of reasoning. Anyway.

The concept of trickling and cascading thoughts to actions based on positivity measurements weighed against the events in history, as well as in the now, is a useful tool. We can only feel something deep if we see it, feel it, touch it, smell it and sense it, and then we can express it. If you see the demographics of one person act negatively against another, we form a framework to interpret future events. The same as positivity in polarity would measure. This applies just the same as we look through our own pupils into the eyes of another or look out into the world for open interpretation.

Fight or flight. What does it do? You can see the pupil and iris of an eye focus, as the long lens of a camera, when fight or flight take effect. When you fear, as an active emotion, a pupil can dilate to absorb more light and thus information to act accordingly for survival or self-protection. When emotion is lost, or fear is absent, no such thing occurs. You can even see the look in the eyes of an addict when they are either using a substance that is manipulating their emotional state or if they are feeling the need to use a dependent substance. By no action of the universe itself, a substance can manipulate emotion and thus reason and logic.

The applicable attribute in our study here is just this. A negative thought acted upon and accepted by another as a positive thought acts to incur negative effect upon those a demographic is attributed to. A terrorist, whether domestic or insurgent, thinks and acts this way to grow the rate at which a virus can spread or an infinitesi-mole's ability to reach out into space and time. Just as the center of our mole is based in Iraq and Syria, growth by way of gravitational waves through unbeknownst civilian populations causes friction and violence by no other cause than the virus of a thought.

Then, do gravitational hairs exist as observed? You tell me. Sure, perhaps the physics would not agree as it is explained, but what then is explained? You look into a hole to see what is in it. You look out from a hole to see what is out. The perceptive points of reference are not the same. You can see the darkness looking into a hole as light diminishes. You can see the light at the end of a tunnel looking upward as darkness is consumed. The terrorist acts that have occurred in years past are measured in this way. One looks into a hole and thinks how this could be instead of looking outward to know why. Not to say an act is mathematically and philosophically justified but only measured and perhaps predictable.

What happens in the event a star goes supernova and has enough energy to form a supermassive black hole or infinitesi-mole? The properties of the universe are inverted, where energy outward becomes energy inward toward one infinitely dense point in space and time. That is our biggest fear in the collapse of humanity as we know it. In a short moment in time, enough energy is created in the clash between entities that particle friction surpasses max capacity to mitigate the residual effect. That is when darkness overwhelms light. It can happen to an individual as well as a society as a group of collective individuals where the sum of all equal parts is not greater than the sum of the whole.

The Economics of Involvement

Before we jump into the melting pot of measurements to look into the rest of the world, let us first look into the eyes of our cause and effect of Middle East resource and ideology conflict. Oil, sure, a valuable and necessary resource. I appreciate the fight for renewable resources to dominate the market, but at this moment in time, it is not possible. We are years away. Sure, the environment would begin to repair itself, but what about society? If a renewable resource has high-value demand, what is to say that would not instigate conflict? If you placed solar panels in the Middle East and labeled this renewable resource with higher relative value than any other around the world, you think bloodshed ceases, and the fire is subdued? Humanity and society as a whole are not that simple.

Below is a chart of armed conflict associated with the price of oil reaching back seventy years in history. The letters mark major conflicts that correlated to a change in the direction of barrel price. We cannot say with 100% absolute certainty at this point if correlation is directly aligned between cause and effect, but we can use our imagination to hypothesize a scenario it is and perhaps measure a rate of involvement based on our understanding of our imaginary value (i).

What we should note in the movement from duality rule in conflict through time into hyper-tense proxy conflict is the increased rate and change in the direction of oil indexes. After WWII, a steady decline in price per barrel is noted until the Cold War reaches its height and ideology conflicts fueled by proxy involvement and proctor intent begin to spin reality. More complex variables are added with each year that passes, and every rocket fired.

Through supply and demand, we should think about proctor versus proxy control of territorial resources. You can see during times of internal conflict within a nation, such as the Iranian revolution, that friction between inhabitant groups complicates resource extraction. This is when the price is at its highest and begins to fall. You can also see, such as during the Gulf War in the late 80s and early 90s, oil value begins to peak. A superpower is directly involved with boots on the ground. You can also look into the 2010-2011 timeframe as the US begins to withdraw a portion of troops and the Arab Spring begins. To this point, internal conflict within the confines of borderlines in the sand correlates with a peak price in oil just as it begins to drop. In proxy conflict in Saudi Arabia, sectarian insurgents threaten and murder western diplomats and oil conglomerate representatives as aggression toward western ideology.

Worrying to note is the drop in oil price during the COVID-19 pandemic as production decreased with a glutton of oil and decreased global demand. What happens when a valuable product drops to the bottom? It begins to climb. Just as the Persian Gulf conflict remains a crisis, perhaps because this is a product of high supply waiting for demand to eat away at the available resource, as the global economy wakes up, let us hope a major conflict does not result from climbing prices, consumption increase, and scramble for control and optimization protocol to grab what is most valuable at the most opportune time. What you should think mostly about this graph other than peaks and valleys is how long a superpower controls the channel of exports during multiple static moments in time when resource value increases and how many of those same points in time does internal conflict prevent extraction when value is decreasing. During the Persian Gulf war, as George H. W. Bush was president, how many of those years did the US control all exports from subjected Arab nations, and at what point during our exit did value drop. It is not so much the cost at one point in time because, as we know, time is fluid, and so is value fluctuation. The question you should ask yourself is, what is the trend that causes action or extraction in correlation with increased resource and commodity value?

In our wrap-up of African proxy involvement, we noted the rate at which a proctor can spin the proxy particle through ideology and resource channel manipulation and the differentiation between intent of both parties. As the Cold War continues and the civil war in Lebanon begins, we too begin to spin. The unstable up and down of oil indices can hypothetically be directly correlated and measured with increased proxy spin. The only thing that cools conflict is unwrapping necessity tied to a resource or ideology. Surprisingly enough, how much tension have you seen in the news between the US and Arab nations or within Arab nations? Not surprising at all. Yeah, small armed conflict exists in relative terms to full-frontal assault by a western superpower or between Saudi or Indian forces against Iran or other nations that align with nationalist control and theocratic fundamentalism. If I didn't work a 60-hour weekday job, I would do this math for you. However, I would rather have you think of it in a state of wonder than the blanket of *here you go.*

Melting Pot of Measurements: A Globe Involved

Any one transaction can apply economically cohesive or adhesive principles where continuity in dealing is kept, or a splash is left with residual decay and evaporation bi-product as an inevitability. Just as a caveman invented the wheel for utilization, so will we. As we leap into a melting pot of the rest of the world as it applies to entity involvement, we can steal something alluded to in *Volume 2* to show our resourcefulness and ability to use any tool analogously in our explanation.

The caveman invented the wheel, supposedly. Our perception of the world drew colors around a similar wheel. We, for simplicity, will use that same primary color wheel to measure economic and ideological balance in trade and even conflict. Instead of drawing the complex figures presented in measuring points in time during proxy involvement between European nations in the continent of Africa, we will simplify this on balance between prismatic color spectrums. In *Volume 2*, we subtly used the duality representation of the color wheel to show the two-dimensional principles of a two-party system. Polarity expands, and colors become deeper red or blue and less simply people looking for whatever truth really exists.

Presented in the previous chapters here as well is the term viscosity, which is alliterated in our use of this color wheel. Primary colors will be used, but secondary colors as dimensions increase as involvement becomes complex in nature. Black and white is not a spectrum we can use when we no longer trade four cows for seven chickens. The value and commodity market mixed with an ideological and political theatre of a protagonist asserting an advantage over the other creates this complexity. A cow is worth sating hunger but when trade affects the global setting and scheme between, one simple trade is not as simple when it is at the behest of millions of individuals as a diplomatic strategy to maintain prominence.

What we also introduced above are the terms: worm, infinitesi-mite, and infinitesi-mole. These terms will be used to define sectors and subsections of one entity that acts for collective personal gain and against opposing entity advantage. The terms as well will be what manipulates our color wheel in balancing the relationship between two or more nations involved in multivariable trade and the correlated cause and effect that can and may result in physical conflict. We must not forget one important concept from our brief analysis of the Cold War; energy is never lost, and friction is either present or inverted. In this thought, we maintain the idea of how a vehicle on our color wheel moves. Spin.

As the World Turns

The irony of Earth as we apply the same concepts present in physics to the meta is that we analogized spherical spin and rotation of one nation involved with another and increased spin associated with multivariable and complex conflicts between proctor and proxy. Isn't the Earth spinning on an axis kind of ironic if you think of the preceding text? If we can measure the United States' involvement in the Middle East or a European Nation's involvement in Africa as the movement through dimensions from one to two to three, isn't it funny that we start with one point and evolve to a sphere that spins? Isn't that what the Earth is as it moves through the vacuum of space? Sure is. And first the Earth was flat, then central, then finally a spinning sphere relative to no central location in the emptiness of space. Our jump from one to two to three is the same process of measurement in war and involvement as it is in our own historical understanding of the Earth as a spatial object to be understood more in depth in time.

The biology of our world is not absent from the same biology present in society and vice versa. The biology of the individual can alliterate the biology of the collective as one body of multifaceted components and chemical and polar charged elements. The macro is the micro. We just add new dimensions that depart from our previous understanding that are essentially the same but with new points of reference as we replace one eye with two or three or more. Looking into the relationship between and among, as either economically based or accelerated resource control in conflict or within the spectrum of both points of reference, we dissect the following:

Trade Agreements

- World Trade Organization
- NAFTA
- European Union
- CAFTA
- Asian Pacific Partnership

Referenced Nations in Involvement: History into Modern Day in Trade and Conflict

- Superpowers: China, Russia, and the US
- North Korea and South Korea
- China, Japan, and the South Pacific
- Turkey and Syria
- Iran, Saudi Arabia, India, and the United States
- Russia, Ukraine, United States, and European Nations
- Iraq, Iran, and Israel
- The United States and Great Britain

World Trade Organization (WTO)

The world trade organization acts as the governing body over all trade agreements between global economic entities involved in the exchange of goods, services, intellectual property, standards, investment that involve entity exchange as import to export, tariff and taxation, sanctions, and other ways in which national economies interact. The most well-known agreements such as NAFTA, CAFTA, and the Asian Pacific Partnership are governed over by this body as effect is placed for and against both and all involved parties. We should note, nothing is non-variable where the weight of dependency and independence can be felt. Every single trade, whether between two individuals with cows and chickens or between multinational entities, places an effect within the spectrum of socioeconomic involvement.

Hundreds of smaller agreements are governed by the WTO that should be noted in the oddities of exchange. One not listed but that we discuss a bit later is trade between Israel and the United States and how that affects the relationship, or non-relationship, with Iran. A cascading of cause and effect then exists in the melting pot of involvement as that relationship also affects the relationships with Saudi Arabia, India, and inevitably the value of commodity exchange across the globe.

Because human nature acts to fight for survival at the expense of the collective for the individual, trade agreements are imperative to our success as a whole. The problem can be thought of as the way in which agreements are upheld and enforced. Because our economy is no longer between two neighbors that live next door and grow fruits and vegetables, the complexity of cash flow through every nook and cranny of the globe is variably impactful. The trade agreements between central America and the United States affect the export value of corn or tobacco in Europe or Asia. If an agreement under the WTO asserts a price or tax on exchange, priority trade is exposed, and buyers and sellers will look elsewhere if exchange export value is not optimized for both parties.

Suppose tomatoes are purchased for $1 a piece by the United States from Central America, as agreed upon under a WTO agreement. In that case, that does not mean Central America won't look elsewhere if they can sell and maintain a higher margin selling a tomato for $1.05 a piece. You may think, what's $0.05? Billions, if not trillions of tomatoes, are cultivated and consumed every year. That adds up.

The WTO, like our hourglass model as a fundamental, is to encapsulate an open system to ensure balance is maintained under the rule of law. But, what about natural law? The effort in governing over global exchange is exactly the same as our approach and the sibling of an economy twinned with society. As we look into entity involvement and viscosity impact and advantageous prowess, a few resources will be needed: legality in trade through tariff and taxation, GDP of each entity, market share of traded commodity, and the ratio of import to export between and among all parties. These traits of trade characterize a cohesive or adhesive alliance measurable as the biological relationship between entities and chain sequence of supply and demand through space and time.

In trade, resources are the control object. In conflict, society is the control object. In commerce, and agreement, invasion is prevented by the cohesive terms of trade and exchange for input and output systems to maintain. The war is not in the force in a spatial vector but the energy of time as space is moved. Because a common goal is established in agreement, our Super Bumper analogy exists departing from trojan virus or mitotic splitting entity involvement.

A Super Bumper is an event between two involved entities with strong cellular walls that protect what is within. Internal components do not enter the genetic construct of another entity but energy between acts to manipulate not source code but the orbital path of an entity mass. The relative strength of each entity along the spectrum of superpower status, decides if involvement is as a bumper or invasive virus. Walk tall and carry a big stick. Tall and strong castle walls both intimidate but protect. Intimidation is nothing without action of force but a castle wall is shown to do its job once one nation thinks they can penetrate through. Two castles with massive reinforcements respect one another, at least enough to know a fight is not worth the energy as ensured destruction is guaranteed.

Any event in trade then weighs a relative measure of bump without invasive coding to re-replicate and re-transcribe another's genetic makeup. Trade between China, Russia and the United States in our multiverse is a system of entities super bumping one another in different directions without complete manipulation of genetic properties. Energy is created to shift but not alter. Trade agreements between larger and smaller nations have a few different characteristics. Because economic agreements are for the success of both parties, physical force is not exchanged but force and energy do exist. In involvement, a larger nation will break the cell walls of a smaller nation just enough for fusion to begin. In this way, the smaller nation is along for the ride. Genetic coding is not changed in one quick motion but very slowly as the two nations now linked move through space in an orbital path around reason.

Our spectrum between conflict in arms and cohesion in trade is then a color wheel measuring the time and space given and taken as mass entities dynamically change from interaction. A trojan substance between Russia and China, is a non variable relative to the size and strength of our cell body. A trojan substance of Russia against Ukraine is much more invasive. Russia and Ukraine will never "bump" because one's cell walls break, and to which viral virus spread occurs. Cohesiveness can be found between Russia and Ukraine in a give and take economic trade agreement in recognition of borders between, but Russia's size will determine the inevitable orbital path of both nations fused together. Think about this concept as we head into our individual agreements.

North American Free Trade Agreement (NAFTA)

As we jump into NAFTA between the United States, Canada, and Mexico, I want you to think of one specific question as we look from different perspectives and analyze the causal relationship between parties: Should the *price* be controlled or the *cost*? Remember this while we move into the explanation of first what NAFTA is and then what the end result becomes.

On January 1, 1994, NAFTA placed market effects on industry producers and manufacturers between the three North American nations to quell the discomfort of trade between nations in close proximity. NAFTA acted in the early 1990s to phase out tariffs and taxes on imports and exports from the US to Mexico, from Mexico to the US, from Canada to Mexico, and from Mexico to Canada. The agreement places little to no effect against US and Canada trade because the United States and Canada free trade agreement (CFTA) holds authority in trade specifically between the two nations. If anything, NAFTA maintains high standards of labor conditions and environmental sustainability to which Canada and the United States are bonded and not necessarily the cost logistics of trade.

Like most topics we discuss, we will try to stay in the middle. Why? Because there are both good and bad traits associated with trade agreements in how they are written and how they are applied. What is important for us is the measurement of cooperation and involvement and the scale to which economic cohesion acts to bring two separate nations together instead of pushing spatial entities apart and creating friction, heat, and conflict in fission. Corn, avocados, tomatoes, vehicles, shoes, textiles, minerals, bell peppers, cucumbers, sugar, dairy powder, pork, beef, beer, plastics, soybeans, fuels, and electronics, to name a few, are traded between all three nations. Trillions of dollars are spent each year between import and export commodity trade within this agreement, but we must look to see where we were before 1994 to understand why we are where we are today.

Incredibly unbalanced tariff taxes on products going into and coming out of Mexico, more than Canada, restricted economic growth by suppressing manufacturing, agricultural, and services industries. Some benefit from pre-NAFTA trade that also lost value and market share post-NAFTA application. As 50% of most tariffs were eliminated on day one, others were phased out. By 2008, a purely free but conditional market was established. The positives of free-market trade, with conditions and restrictions, are seen, but side effects against the relative market state pre-NAFTA are felt. If caveman Sam and caveman Mike never invented the word tariff and the applicable definition of restricting but profiting off trade between entities, no residual would be felt post-NAFTA.

Every cause has an effect where every action has an opposite and equal reaction. We want to look into the question provided in the first sentence of this subsection: Should the *price* be controlled or the *cost?* The majority part of this volume digs into involvement through conflict. But, how do we build and fuse a bridge across a border and make sure even flow from each polar opposite direction maintains homeostasis and bridge maintenance is kept up with equal and equitable input from each party? Through time and space, wear and degradation are inevitable, just as growth is. Just as nuclear energy creates radiation, we must constantly maintain our system and contain and mitigate any residual effect even if growth is massive. One can grow strong and healthy and go to the gym and build muscle, becoming a mountain of a person, but one malignant cell, unnoticed or untreated, can cripple the life of the strongest human.

For illustrated understanding, let's look at the figure of a bridge below. This is the NAFTA Gate bridge, where each binary involved entity is subject to maintaining support beams to ensure it does not fall and cohesion falters. Even as NAFTA is a trilateral agreement, trade between each nation remains bilateral. A road across a bridge is only two ways across our expansion; NAFTA would almost be allegorical to the police on the road on each side to ensure nefarious actions are not ignored.

The purpose of creating a bridge is that carrying millions of pounds of goods across a body of water by boat is not efficient if an expansion bridge can reach the other side. Of course, ships travel from San Francisco to China every day, but when space between two nations is small, optimization is finding a simple technological solution. God forbid we had one channel, and a ship gets stuck sideways blocking all goods from being delivered. Of course, you can always have a car accident on a bridge, but the damage is not too much to clean up and clear the channel of trade, and the cost is not as high either.

In our figure, how do we decide who maintains what and how we control the path that is equitably used and able to be accessed? That is somewhat of a big question. If we look at static points in history leading from NAFTA's implementation, what are the negative aspects, and then how can they be mitigated? As tariffs are removed, value is funneled to different entities producing the same products, all to open a free market and lower the price of consumer goods. Are we then worried about the price or the cost? What is the cost of cultivating avocados? What then is the price? What about any other commodity in trade? Is it a Darwinist economic policy that the lowest cost garners the highest bidder? Or the product always goes to the highest bidder? Well, that is the genetics of our optimization by individual path to success. How does an arbitrary agreement affect what was and what is? The answer is not skilled or low-skilled labor, as some may have you believe, but costly and low-cost labor. If someone has to pay a higher dollar amount to make a pair of shoes than someone that will accept lower pay and make the same shoe, which one are you going to pay to manufacture shoes? It is a simple answer. Even if we may not notice when we go shopping, or maybe we might, it is not because a low or high-skilled worker made the product that NAFTA affected, but that the low-skilled worker's cost, not their pay, is higher and standard of living is much lower.

In equity terms, if the status quo for a worker in Mexico is to work under low health standards and few high-skilled jobs or training for those jobs, the correlation between exchange in goods weighs heavier. What we established in *Volume 1* is in a class system, equity is curved and non-linear. Because a worker in the United States gets paid $15 an hour to work at McDonalds, rent is equitably and relatively lower than someone that works in Mexico and gets paid $7.50 an hour. If the cost to rent for the US worker is $1000 a month, and the cost for the worker in Mexico is $700 a month, lower equitable wages and standard of living are felt. The difficulty is even though NAFTA promises health and labor standards, no one governing body with any power to do anything is going to tell either nation they are doing something wrong to force them to increase their standard because self-governance in trade is agreed not enforced or even really enforceable. That is especially true if general motors see they can get away with US Labor violations in a foreign country untaxed by importing products across the border at a lower cost. Low cost means higher margin. But, at a cost to who? So then, what does an agreement look like that ensures equity cost in production and not only tradable price? Well, GM would expense the same cost per vehicle manufactured in Mexico as they would in Detroit. They also should.

In our figure below, we have two sides of an expansion bridge which both parties in a bilateral agreement of control over but in different ways. As we discussed the transit freeway system in *Volume 2*, this idea is very similar, but instead of one controlling entity, we have the relationship between two entities policed by one unified body but officers of two. The laws of the road described in the previous volume still stand. The polar relationship between production and consumption is the same but what we want to look at is why and how, and then how many companies or countries are encouraged to produce a good or service on the other side of the border and why.

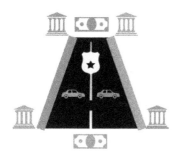 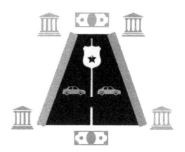

What we see here is balance. Even though this book is in black and white, you can still see the shaded darkness of what is blue and red. Because both are equal in this causal relationship, it is irrelevant to know which is actually red or blue but notice the difference in shade. For the US, on one side of the equation, they maintain one pillar while Mexico maintains the other. At the same time, one maintains the expansion, and the other maintains the suspensions holding the bridge up. It is important in this relationship that both keep to the bargained deal because if the expansion falls, the suspension supporting it will not hold and if the suspension breaks, the expansion will not hold. Just as any pillar that falls, the bridge collapses regardless of who's fault.

As we looked then to the depiction of a roadway, we talked in *Volume 2* about barriers preventing vehicles from falling off a cliffside. This is the same scenario as both entities involved in maintaining our bridge are responsible for ensuring our exports and imports make it to the supposed destination. Without this, the risk of production catastrophe for one industry or the other adds to volatility in trade. At the end of our road, we have toll booths like how we have to pay bridge tolls (even if the proposal to fund our bridge through community means is already paid for and bridge tolls continue). This would signify a system of tariffs. As imports come in, this is the point at which an entity would apply a tariff. Before an export exits one nation at the border, this would then be when one nation applies an export tariff. The police badge in the middle should appear as a different shade and is supposed to be yellow. As an independent entity to oversee logistics and the agreement is followed, this would be NAFTA presiding over both systems as production input and output in commodity trade move across the expansion.

What then would the pillars, expansion of the bridge, and the suspension cables be? Well, simply put, the intangible characteristics to safe and healthy means of production. These would include labor laws, dedication to fair wages, equal pay and opportunity, health and human services for those in production sectors, and benefits or welfare for working citizens. What we don't see in the balancing of this equation is deterioration, but I can guarantee its presence. How so? What makes a road deteriorate? Usage. As the United States is a massive importer of goods and services, they are also an exporter of manufacturing jobs of products to then be imported. This balance never ends well because one side of the road is used more than the other, and potholes are formed. It is easy for one company to drive across the bridge once and then send all their vehicles the other way hundreds of times a week.

In global economic trade terms, the issue we see is a trade deficit at the expense of the workers on both sides of the border. Sure, more jobs are created in Mexico, but that does not mean the individual standard of living for each individual increases. The collective may increase a bit, but the equity attained by each new job does not increase. Production overall increases, and so does GDP in Mexico, but again that does not mean a "low-skilled" job is prioritized. Instead, this job is re-prioritized from "high-skilled" labor to low-skilled wages simply with the flip of a switch. During the transition to NAFTA, low-skilled labor in the US was 14% of the workforce and 72% of the working population in Mexico. High-skilled labor was 34% and 12%, respectively. The question then remains, what is your definition of skilled labor? Cost. Do not follow this next assumption directly, but an artist that creates a masterpiece and is only paid $15 for a week's work would be assumedly a low-skilled laborer. I would not imagine low-skilled labor is anything other than a dollar sign associated with a title because we would be too lazy to itemize what each job description is and the "skill" required. Inversely, if the same painting were created anywhere else in the world for $1,500,000, who are you going to buy it from? Exactly. You are going to spend less on the same masterpiece, especially if a name is left from it. A Da Vinci painting is a Da Vinci whether or not it was created under one governing authority or another.

The point being, what is the cost of "low-skilled" labor? The equity available to the laborer as well as the curve to which labor standards are applied. Just as the analogy presented in previous volumes, someone simply needing income is more likely to work under harsh working conditions. If laws then do not support human rights, how is a citizen that doesn't know different going to act? As if this is normal. The curve in equity always aligns with not only a standard of living but the privilege to live. If you were to tell someone starving to death to punch their friend, or something worse, for $100, they have a higher chance of nefarious acts if it quells their insatiable hunger. The same principle applies. Low-level needs, assigned by Maslow's hierarchy, are there for a reason.

The truth, however, is this hierarchy should not be a pyramid that maintains natural law; only some receive fulfillment needs. If we were to measure this pyramid in one static moment in time, our similar curved hourglass model would exist. It is not that the edges of this pyramid are wrong but that they should be curved to a point and more rigid. In reality, this process to fulfillment is a circle and spiral to the center where different needs are met simultaneously outward to inward, but that is another book to be written.

What is noted, similar to the conflict vacuum of the Middle East during the United States' withdrawal from Iraq and Syria, the economic impact is similar to the chaos of removing containment walls. As containment is reduced, free trade is conditioned, the withdrawal of containment borders punctures a very tiny hole in the vacuum of each industry involved. From 1994 to 2008, the trade deficit with Mexico has increased because we naturally import more than we export. Nearly 700,000 jobs are lost in this interaction. The problem, though, Mexico is not benefiting. Select individual conglomerates are. We may feel more equal but we are less equitable. A hole in your vacuum always leaks residual loss of equity in an economic vector of space, weakening both parties by instability through frictions between balanced cause and effect.

NAFTA Involvement Depicted

Does it make sense to increase means of production only by arbitrarily opening the door to cheaper production in relative terms to past market input to output? The question to follow is who, what, where, and how are logistics in play utilized? Who benefits from low-cost means of production? What is being produced, and what barriers of trade are present to benefit both sides of the production cost and price equation and contain residual effects? Where are manufacturers benefiting most, and what natural laws are bypassed simply by the location of production? How is this process manipulated for the benefit of one at the expense of most, or how can this process of manipulation be removed?

All important questions. The logistics of free trade agreements bring an additional dimension into play. Normally production by A for A is simple. Production by A for B brings our three-dimensional process of measurable involvement to the forefront of quantifying, through analogy, to illustrate our reality. Real quantifiable data can also be applied to see the numbers for ourselves, but first, we must hypothesize. When we do get there, what numbers do you think we would use? Where measuring involvement in conflict is difficult to quantify absolutely, the quantifiability of involvement through solely economic measurements is much easier. Simply, numbers are available attached to dollar signs.

GDP, tariff rate, import to export ratio, standard of living, poverty rate, labor costs, trade deficit, job displacement, and more. Just as the difficulty in measuring the emotion felt of an insurgent or effect on a civilian in the Middle East, the difficulty is to quantify labor conditions and standard of living. Sure, we can measure the normal income required to maintain the basic standard of living above poverty in each class, but it is much more difficult to measure the ability for an individual to thrive in relative terms to another, creating a similar product in two different countries with two different "standards of living." Equity ratios can be guessed, but how can we measure the state of success and emotional response of one individual in a group of individuals through the effect of trade? You can, but again, it's very difficult. You should expect a complete analogous equation for that model from me in due time, but it won't be present here. We are looking at the hard numbers in this phase, even if we only do directly apply a few of them here.

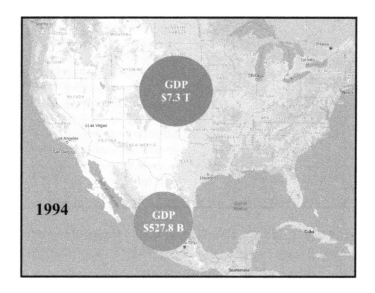

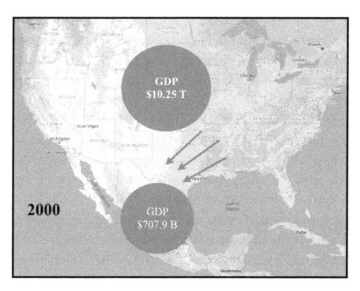

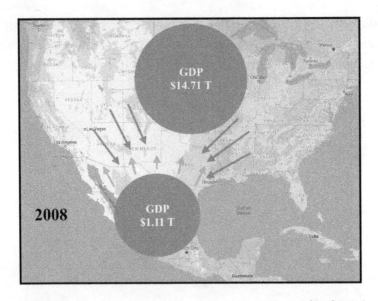

Before we look directly at each of the three stages of before, during, and after as it relates to cause and effect, let's think of one idea. If the standard of living and labor standards are not ideal and production increases exponentially, where are people going to want to go? In this situation, North. Standard of living is then anything from income, cost of food, and living expense, and then protection by the law or protection from the law. In Mexico, sometimes the law can be the enemy, and sometimes a cartel is the law and in a barbaric, blood-stained, and cutthroat way.

In 1994, the United States GDP was just about $7 Trillion while Mexico's GDP was just above $500 Billion. We know other variables are in the equation, such as other exporters and importers for both sides from other nations. If we imagine these variables are equal and canceled out and the causal relationship between these two entities is bilateral entanglement, then we can try to justify the end result through logic. The US is the number one importer from Mexico and imports 76% of all Mexican exports in 2021. GDP in the United States is less dependent on Mexico just for the simple fact of population and market size. An inverted trade deficit, even though not directly correlated to raw dollars, the size of the United States to Mexico would crush our southern ally. The trade deficit in 2019 of $98.5 Billion would cripple a country whose GDP is roughly $1.1 trillion. Perhaps a few years of this imbalance could be absolved but imagine if a 10% trade deficit to total GDP each year since 1994 were the effect. Just as absolution is achieved by stagnation or catastrophe, there are two different reasons citizens would flee to our southern border. One, rampant production under unsustainable conditions or two, stagnation and degradation by means of economic collapse from absent production. Both equal one thing; a sense of *protection* outside and beyond the wall of relatively felt *control.*

When jobs go in, but people come out, that is not a good sign. The process in which agreements of this magnitude, even if the fine print is perfect, must be followed and governed accordingly. It is easy for an American company to move into Mexico and abandon United States labor standards but much more difficult for a company from Mexico or even a Mexican citizen to make it to the United States to produce a good or service. Where our labor standards are above and beyond adequate, Mexican citizens avoid confrontation with employers because working conditions, as well as standard of living and safety in general, are still a step above in the US. What do we do, though? An employer still has the ability to pay a "South of the Border wage" in the US for undocumented and even some documented workers. Again, why? Our friends that have moved into the United States are simply happier to be here and don't want to risk returning to conditions south of the border, whether *right or wrong* or lawful or not. Whether the law is followed here or there or followed by anyone for everyone anywhere is apparently a parent acting, un-apparently? A conundrum. NAFTA. Human nature for exploitation.

A Bridge Over Troubled Waters: Cohesive vs. Adhesive

Before we move to the next agreement, let's define more thoroughly what a bridge represents in our analogy and interpretation. Fundamentally, a bridge is an expansion over water so land vehicles can travel across. It is neither movement over land nor movement over the surface of water but both. To transport something on or under the surface of water requires a boat, submarine, or Maritime vessel absent of wheels. Society, in large part, acts to produce goods and services on land where a body of water acts as a trivial barrier to the movement of land-based goods and services. The task of transporting goods by train or automobile and then onto a ship is a task in itself. Bridges are useful to close the distance of space and time over a body of water using terrain-based vehicles. This may seem simple, and you may wonder why this is important. The truth is it is very important. The reason being, technological advancement to close the gap in space and time through cooperative principles allows us to eliminate a barrier to delivering our output product.

Our understanding is that a bridge will always connect separate entities with one common barrier between them by means of cooperation and technological advancements. It would be odd to shape a three-way bridge because that is somewhat impractical. Possible, if the geography allows such a wonder but highly improbable. Not only would it be hard to build a bridge in three directions, but we would, in this case, have to build a three-way road as well if we really wanted to accomplish this task. Perhaps flying cars would solve this problem in an instant but let's not go there. At least not yet.

As the symbolism of connecting two separate entities by one common and cohesive goal, we have a bridge, and bridges are used throughout history as this same symbol. WWII in both European and Pacific theatre had armies using bridges strategically to gain an advantage. Why? Again, just as above, land vehicles don't do too well with a mile-wide river between landmasses. As Germany or the Allies are able to control an outpost or output point, progress for the other is blocked. In retreat, Allies or Nazis would "burn bridges" or strap C4 to the supports and bring the expansion down to buy time as their retreat creates space between.

The symbol of expansion and humanity's achievement of manifest destiny to explore all corners of the world is one bridge on the West Coast, the Golden Gate. Where cohesion is present, the process between trade and mutually inclusive benefit is kept intact. When adhesion is applied, cohesion once was the goal. If we are to look at further trade agreements or the NAFTA we described above, what would you see in the condition of our bridge? Cohesion pre-NAFTA was not a thought. Adhesion was a small solvent against trade progression, but the barrier between them created a difficulty of crossing over troubled waters. NAFTA was building a bridge as one of the largest free markets ever to have been formed. However, maintenance is now required, and without proper channels of maintaining support beams, suspension wire, and expansion side walls, adhesiveness will appear. So then the question again, what do you see in NAFTA from 1994 to today? Adhesion is present as the inverse effect of cohesion being replaced.

While energy is never destroyed, it can certainly be misplaced. If our trade agreement were to maintain absolute balance and equilibrium over time, the sticky strings of our duct tape adhesive would not exist. As we rip the tape off, our strings in the NAFTA agreement are the residue and residual effect of the agreement itself; jobs leaving the United States and immigrants flooding to the border. Where cost of goods sold can be optimized at the expense of the worker, jobs will leave for capital optimization, but civilian workers will return by inequitable and unequal health and labor standards relative to the inversely involved entity to which the agreement is made and effected upon in causal relation.

The difficulty is in analogizing an expansion bridge in these terms, but we must grasp this thought. Two different vectors of space exist, where one is over land and one over water. Transportation over water requires a different field state, of input to output, than if we were traveling over land. Optimization in the exchange of two proximally close entities exists if a barrier of input to output is removed. Both parties in this solution require cohesion. Adhesion brings the barrier back into play.

Any relationship begins with the desire for cohesiveness. Just as our study looks into the rapid change in mass and not only distance of space and time, adhesiveness can become the residual. Genetically, as involvement begins, this can be a predetermined path and inevitably. Or, one simple line of coding fueled by a malignant accelerant can create the same effect and due cause. Our effort in linking two sides in cohesion is awareness, understanding, and a mutually inclusive sum of two individual parts. An expansion over troubled waters requires cohesion because the risk of failure is higher and more consequential.

A bridge between worlds is then the interconnecting bilateral pathway creating a network of cohesive links just as a spider's web. Awareness and understanding of the balance between two entities linked together solve the underlying foundational faults. If the teetering of instability is corrected between all two-way relationships, then the sum unbalance of all relationships as a whole is resolved. In our trilateral agreement of NAFTA, we see this duality focus affecting a trilateral relationship. The governing authority does not think of this three-way bridge because it is impossibly difficult to govern over uniquely different relationships. What we do notice is the framework for mutually inclusive trade along a two-way street where foundational rules govern a trilateral framework. If a triangle were imagined, the focus is on each expanse between two points to ensure the whole trinity is strong. This is our same thought.

European Union (EU)

Following both World War I and II, Europe is left in shambles. Both figuratively or physically and economically or infra-structurally, most nations are left rebuilding from the effects of war. Looking back to Africa and the Middle East, rebuilding in Europe is a bit different. Why? Because it actually happens. Where the continent and Africa and the Middle East may have small improvements to society, the European Union allows cohesive principles to grow exponentially after the destruction that ensued from armed physical conflict. The simple idea is that if the bombs never stop, it is hard to build. The European Union is the most important agreement with the most positive effect in human history. One may think the logistics behind the EU are troublesome, but I would disagree. Sure, perhaps the UK supports other European Nations more than some causing BREXIT, but that is beside the point.

Every family has a big brother that pulls more weight than most. It is the family life of nations in close proximity and simply that. If one does not pull a little bit more weight than a weaker sibling, even the family falls apart. If a big brother does not work two jobs while their single parent is sick, then who in their family is going to eat? No one. If the big brother doesn't work and food is not on the table, who is going to act by survivalist measures and levels of Maslow's hierarchy and be angry by simply being hungry? Everyone. Now, it should be noted, equity weight should maintain a balance between nations. However, it is more important to make sacrifices economically so that sacrifices aren't made both politically and physically. If the EU were not formed, a third war in the European landscape would have happened in the 1970s. No question about it. The Cold War would not have remained a Cold War. Friction with proximal effect would have increased the temperature. An alliance in Europe could very measurably depict why the United States is what it is. You may think this to be an ambiguous stretch, but I will tell you it is the truth.

Economic relationships are a precursor to conflict or the beginning of resolve. *Resolute*, the 27 nations of the European Union are a depiction of cohesion at all cost. Sure, adhesive measures are seen but mitigated and arbitrated by big brother explaining the residual if this relationship falls apart. Sure, BREXIT, whatever. The UK still deals in trade with the rest of Europe just now as one entity does with a second where the cohesiveness of all European nations is still a wall against absolution in its inevitability and in its entirety. We discussed the wormlike black hole or infinitesi-mole effect of Syria and the Middle East. A decline of the involved relationship among and between all European nations would be catastrophic to the entire world. The retraction, gravitational pull, and residual hairs of the black mole in the Middle East would be minuscule in comparison.

As resources and ideology are accelerants to the origin of conflict between entities, the potency of all European nations at odds would be flammable beyond any energy source ever created. We analogize our system as a rocket engine transporting a shuttle into the upper atmosphere and ideologies and resource control as potency to carry a payload into the stratosphere. In this thought, the dissolution of the European Union is not flipping the engine on and the rocket not firing. It is flipping on the switch and incinerating everything within proximal reach.

Not to input a bit of fear, but this is the honest truth. In *Volume 4*, avoiding absolution, we will dive into those dark depths. In our effort here, we recognize economic relationships as a precursor or foreshadowing of what is to follow. For us, at this moment, we should look at what has been prohibited or avoided instead based on preventing history from repeating itself. As cohesion replaced adhesive principles, a constant war of proximal nations is avoided. Friction is cooled by water, where flammable potency is a hot commodity. A constant source of water prevents the inevitable. The moment our water source turns off, our fire rages to which not end in sight would be apparent. A thin layer or splash against a mirror will never extinguish heat associated with hunger and a fire top stove that always burns with a pot of water sitting atop. Let's compartmentalize the characteristics of our extinguisher.

Union Components and Attributes

Following World War II, economic cooperation became the driving force for unity in Europe, but no formal political unifying agreement was created and installed. Though economic cooperation is mandatory for achieving peace for nations, there was still another piece to the puzzle. Full and unabridged political unity is the other. Where dollars, or Euro, signs are important, they mean nothing if dignity is lost. Creating one single market is important, but residuals are felt if aligning standards are not attributed just as our NAFTA example. If the dignity of the individual is lost, what work is the dignity promised? An internal fight would only amass out of external belief. What is prosperity if the interpreter idealizes the prosperity promised a few miles away? The purpose of the EU is to encompass all facets of market system theory and societal importance and relevance at the individual and multi-state level. Democracy, through European parliament as a parliament of parliaments, to govern trade and contribution to the collective is a necessity.

Trade, Humanitarianism, and Diplomacy are the three heads of authority but also incapacitation. Trade is ensured internally between and among nations by forming the euro and lightning border restrictions for products to pass back and forth. Imagine driving from San Francisco to San Diego to sell a loaf of bread, and you cross three countries with individual currencies along the way. A nightmare. Every stop you make costs you time until your bread spoils. If you wanted to sell your bread in one country, the process in which you pay taxes or convert currency revenue costs more than the loaf itself in time and effort. Just as a bridge over troubled waters, the EU removes an unnecessary but genetically placed barrier. By removing mostly all borders, ingenuity is possible where time is spent building as opposed to protecting or navigating a stream of waterfalls and pitfalls or roads of potholes or falling rocks. It's easier to get to your destination if a boulder doesn't crush your vehicle, or you have to stop every few hundred miles to show your passport or go through customs.

From Europa.eu, European goals are listed to "promote peace and well-being. Offer freedom, security, and justice without internal borders. Sustainable development based on balanced economic growth and market economy combat social discrimination, promote scientific progress, enhance economic, social, and territorial *cohesion*. Respect cultural diversity. Establish an economic and monetary union whose currency is the Euro." Of course, cohesion. Biology speaks for itself. An effort of inclusion, without barriers that drive entities apart, is just this. A border weighed heavier than another's will only shut the door to both sides. Internal fluidity in Europe promotes this principle. The moment one nation closes to another is the first step in all borders closing and a Jenga tower falling. Imagine pulling a block from the center as if Germany closed itself to the outside world again. All the pieces are to fall. Perhaps not immediately, but eventually. Disruption then aligns with natural law. In conflict, space dictates who is what, and time dictates how and when. Conflict in close proximity will mostly segregate into A verse B. Just as our b-racketeering approach in *Volume 2*, small conflict will always add up to one final battle. We can look back to World War I as small wars between nations begin, but inevitably Europe devolves into an axis versus allies. All axises added to a sphere create spin. An arbitrary axis creates arbitrary spin unfounded, normally, in true environmental realities and parameters. The greater or lesser evil is a devil always driving a hard bargain. *All other statistics are pulled from data.wto.org, state.gov/usrelations, and census.gov/foreigntrade.*

The EU acts as one Humanitarian body that represents diplomacy for all European nations around the world. Sure, some nations act individually with other alliances but not outside the framework of the EU. Britain is a strong ally to the United States, as are France and Germany. Previously in history, perhaps not so much. The EU sends diplomats to other nations for political purposes as well as to act as conflict security strategists. However, it is difficult for EU boots on the ground to act proctor because an act of conflict by one, in this case, is an act of conflict by all. The EU very heavily aligns with the idea of diplomacy and security as opposed to actions of an aggressor in conflict. This means simply the term "do not fire unless fired upon" is very much the approach. EU forces are normally present during conflict to help protect fleeing refugees as opposed to fighting on the front lines. We have proxy armies for that.

The Curse in Precursors

What someone doesn't know won't hurt them is somewhat true. We do not know an army on Mars exists if they do, but they may, and they could invade Earth. Well, hypothetical, to say the least, but applicable. Whether Martians are waiting just past the moon or not does us no harm at the moment, but harm could be present in the near future. Whether Will Smith can save us from invasion is not the question. The question is, what are we going to do when we become aware of volatility from one involved entity?

When nations become involved in economic and political authority, there are only two outcomes. Similar to the difference between pure capitalism and pure socialism is that either we absolve ourselves into a disaster field state or we apply principle forces that demand the drive toward equilibrium. The process of cohesion in practice is then practical in reasoning every action made within the process and time of involvement. At birth, during replication, when agreements are made, is there malignancy or purity? Because we know friction is created, are we cooling our flame just enough so it doesn't burn the house down, or is there one potent fume that crisps our foundation? Is the energy then we create optimized and contained, or is it born cursed to an inevitable and cataclysmic catastrophe? We do not know until we are aware. That is the problem that holds no solution.

Again, what we do know is what cohesive principles prevent. What we do know is what adhesive principles create. What we can see are adhesive principles that devolve involvement into chaos and collapse. What we can see is cohesion preventing this same devolvement. What we can't see is what happened to a supermassive European single market system of nations that exercised cohesive principles and then dissolved into adhesion and fire. This is both a good thing and a bad thing. It is good because we don't have to watch Europe burn. It is bad because we don't quite know what will happen if it does occur, which I am fine with because I can theorize well enough in preventative measure.

Just as breaking genetic and elementally entangled particles of a hydrogen molecule or atom, massive amounts of energy are created through both fusion and fission. For this, I am fine theorizing. Of course, particles within an atom have polar opposite charges that keep them together. That is how physical mass forms. What we do not apply in physics is what we apply in all of our texts and excerpts, changing mass. When the genetic properties of an entity, whether an atom or a country, are manipulated to the extreme threshold outside our margin of error, massive amounts of energy is created. What happens if the European Union dismantles itself in fire and fury? More than one type of atom is ripped apart or slammed into another. Boom. This is just why we don't play with fire or the physical components of natural law or manipulate life itself. We have a habit of really messing things up and messing with things we shouldn't. I understand; we just wonder too much. But please, leave the atoms alone.

When two or more entities become involved, predestination is set, and a precursor is created. A conceptualization point aligns with genetic makeup and applicable accelerants. A reasonably aware individual in 1984 could likely tell you Brexit would occur at some point. Why? It is very measurable how much more the UK upholds the rest of the continent as big brother becomes tired of doing all the work around the house while their 26 other siblings have grown comfortable in eating without working to pay the bills. Of course, many nations in Europe pull their weight. Analogy aligned; this is a proper example. You get one boisterous sibling and a new girlfriend or spouse, and they have other bills to pay. Granted, this may not align perfectly; ideologies are placed separately from the original framework. If our boisterous sibling feels they are taken advantage of by the rest of the family, whether true or not, decides they have had enough, is that so unexpected? As time goes by, we notice our relative weight of importance as a gravitational shift occurs the moment we become aware, almost as if a dual property paradox arises.

First, we must act or our family starves. We act, and our family is content for a while. Food continues to reach the table. Our family asks for more than what is given as if the weight carried by one is now not enough. Siblings are growing, but input does not. It simply requires more to feed a 14-year-old than it does a seven-year-old. One brother can only provide so much. The 14-year-old asks for more and more. At one point, before, starvation was almost inevitable. Now, being full is not enough. Now we want candy and dessert. My favorite story as a child was "If You Give a Mouse a Cookie, He is Going to Want a Glass of Milk" because it is true. The moment big brother becomes aware of his importance and then in the moment of interpreted ungratefulness, big brother sees opportunity, whether cognitively aware of perceptive intent or not. Just the same, siblings can be more than grateful, but the genetic makeup of big brother will tell you whether or not they leave the situation for the sake of fulfillment or fulfillment of another.

As our big brother is genetically programmed, so is the United Kingdom, and what do we know about genetics in our model? Mass objects change coding with new input as accelerants are added within each measurement in time. Any sort of malignancy can be pumped with a growth accelerant if focused in one area or another. What may have existed as a small protruding node has now become a new mass or fan-able virus. Is Brexit then the product of a cursed precursor not of 2020 but buried deep in the sands of 1958 with one tiny shard of glass laid on the beach for a future unsuspecting person to cut their foot and become infected? Is this cut then just a flesh wound, or is it much worse? Does our entity have their hepatitis shots? We only become aware of our precursor once blood is drawn. Nothing in the future is laid without an egg in the past, where nothing in the past is a hen that doesn't lay an egg for something that is to happen in the future.

Union Involvement and Measurements

Like the involved measurements of the US and Mexico, below are figures of European nations during the early part of union formation, during the height of union expansion, and 2020 during Brexit. GDPs of all nations involved as well as European Union weight and burden sharing are included. Based on our interpretation of the US and Mexico relationship, I want you to think of all the things that have happened through history in this time period that could affect each mass and cause one to grow ahead of another or behind. I want you to think of the weight big brother carries and why they may want to leave a family behind. A prince might flee a family for solitude in the face of uncharacteristically high measures of discomfort. Does one duty to family outweigh the duty of the individual, and is this measure justified in action? Of course, conflict has not arisen in physicality but could it? Could conflict arise from a neighbor because big brother is absent? How does leaving only as a sole provider but staying as a protector affect the status quo? All of these factors and more predict the future. See the figure below.

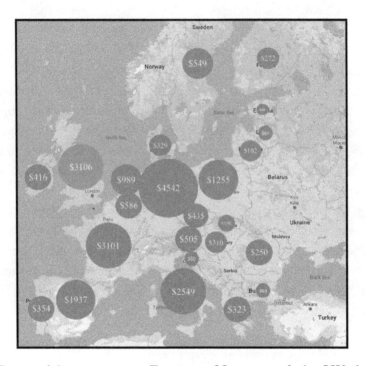

Depicted here are most European Nations and the UK during the point in time when Brexit shaped a new diplomatic relationship among the family of the EU. Listed as well are historical measurements of the GDP of EU nations throughout history that led to this point. We did not create a bubble plot of GDP through time to focus on the relationship of nation to nation GDP to Debt ratios as a strain on family bonds. Historical GDP is listed for reference. As we look through history and focus our intent on this static moment, what can we see, and how can we see it? We know the UK is unsatisfied with footing the bill for other nations and facilitated debt mitigation with states such as Greece and Italy that levy a heavyweight of debt to GDP.

In a family setting, this weight is distributed throughout the household to lighten the burden on one, but the burden is weighed then on the fittest. It is true, if one falls they all fall as a line of dominos. European banks are forced to sell and manage debt bonds to keep Greece, or other nations underwater, from drowning and bringing down the rest of the EU. Sure, we can compare smaller individual GDP in total dollars to the accompanied debt ratio and notice a total dollar sum is not as massive as it would be if a larger producer were equally underwater. The important index we could look at is the GDP-to-Debt ratio per capita to understand the effect upon the individual. Direct correlation is tough to iron out, but metrics can begin to paint that picture.

Just as we mix colors to create a new hue along a spectrum, we should do the same here. GDP is measured in a shade of red, and our debt ratio is measured in blue. You can't really see the color scheme for this book is in black and white but know the polarity of shading acts to mix with the other. Our WVI could equitably measure and mix our color if we were to compare actual GDP with a percentage ratio. You can see the size of our spheres in each diagram. Imagine if you were at home depot or another paint store and the customer service representative was mixing you a color to paint your new house. No debt is good debt, but equal debt is controllable debt. We obviously would like our house to be painted as red as possible. A 0% debt to GDP ratio would have a house in the brightest red hue as possible. A 100% debt to GDP ratio would mix one gallon of blue paint and one gallon of red paint, and our house on the neighborhood block would stand out as very purple. As the scale swings toward out-of-control debt, we begin to bleed a new shade.

In painting the European neighborhood or rooms in a family home, we have two gallons of paint to mix and paint from. Relatively we want to paint our house in pure production and in a deep red shade, even if that is honestly an ugly color for a house. What happens when debt swings out of control? There is no threshold for our blue hue because our system on this end is opened into any potential possibility of catastrophe. The moment we surpass 100% GDP to debt ratio, we begin to replace our red gallon with blue. If we are Greece and hold 199% debt to GDP, we only have one swipe of red paint with our brush left. As we surpass a 2 to 1 ratio, we begin falling into absolution. Our house can only be painted blue, but now we are reducing from 2 gallons back to 1 gallon and then 0 gallons. As blue paint is used, it is not replaced. As time goes on and our house needs new paint, we simply have nothing to paint with—production halts.

Debt is measured against a nation, and bonds are used in such a way that we can only lend and receive assistance until means are exhausted—figured below. As the capacity to pay back loans becomes increasingly more challenging, lenders will refuse to help someone until they help themselves. Tourism, agriculture, and shipping are not enough to foot the bill. If GDP is exhausted and levied against where new tapped resources in any industry are not channeled, lending to or from is unreasonable. The problem, even if a ratio of 1-to-1 is present, interest is the slow bleed of the host. At no point does this bleeding stop unless 100% of GDP is used to pay debt services. That is unreasonable because people need to eat. Interest ensures malignant growth without surgery to remove the mass.

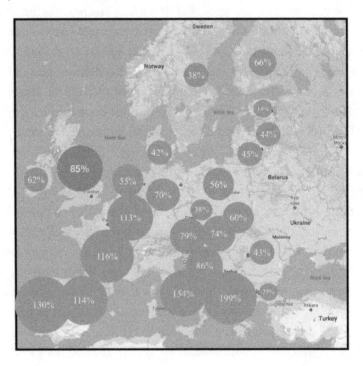

You may wonder why the UK in our figure is blue in one diagram and red in the other but inverse of all other nations. It is that way for a reason, obviously. As the UK removes itself from direct connection to EU diplomacy, they act as a reciprocally involved entity where balance in interaction should be measured as an external influence. Just as debt is measured against the shade of production so is production of the UK measured in balance with EU nations once Brexit becomes law. External measurements should be noticed by the genetic change in a dynamic state of interaction. Even as the UK has direct trade agreements with the EU, imagine the difficulty and complexity of the European theater of trade if all nations decide to pick a color hue and duality is lost. Our bridge over troubled waters succumbs to the ocean, and supports crumble, and suspensions are destroyed.

In the effort of pulling toward and measuring the law of averages to form one product output of entity weight, the UK's removal is just as a subgroup regressing away from the mean. As all sums add and weigh energy potential, both good and bad, of the EU, Britain's detachment does have its genetic effect. Even though alliances are kept while the symbolic representation is lost and cohesion is maintained, for the most part, some adhesive material is added to be removed. Some supports are damaged without the effort of repair or replacement. To the union as an entity, those supports are needed to be shaped by other nations. Our bridge is no longer from the EU out to the rest of the world, but a new one first across the English channel once crossed to defend against evil. In transition, with the Trade and Cooperation Agreements in place, a new bridge is being built.

If we think of wear and tear and maintenance through the collective approach, the UK is responsible for their own maintenance and ensuring the path for imports and exports is open for EU nations. The EU has the same responsibility to sustenance in the same agreement. It is quite unnecessary to create this new bridge but only by diplomatic perception. Britain is an important figure in the EU political theater. Economically, and perhaps factors I have not seen should be contemplated as well, free will allows the dropping of someone else's weight for them to carry. You can't force someone to carry your luggage if they don't want to, no matter how heavy or light you think it is. That is free will.

A multi-national agreement designating each nation separate from the other in close proximity where borders are firm creates friction. As the UK is a big brother leaving home for a new life, imagine if Germany, France, and Italy follow and leave Estonia and Lithuania to fend for themselves, only hoping the neighbor to the North remains friendly. Russia sits and waits, weighing its options for resource control through ideological manipulation and perhaps proxy conflict across Ukraine and into Eastern Europe.

If the balance of territorial integrity is determined by a balanced color wheel encompassing and spinning all hues and shades, the complexity of cooperation would be too much for the vehicle our wheels are attached to. Track back into pre-World War I, and that is what you will have back from history's abyss, returned. As we become closer than ever in time and space, what do you have now that we discussed in proxy conflict? No longer are we simply dualistic in conflict. Speed in a given direction is manipulated no longer by movement through space only but by spinning an object into a new melting pot of reality. All truth is lost if no truth is aligned with collective cooperation. The theater of Europe devolves a prodigy protagonist back into the cursed child.

Country	GDP 1960	GDP 1990	GDP 2020	Debt Ratio 2020	Notes
United Kingdom	$114.52B	$1022.46B	$3106.21B	85%	
Austria	$13.55B	$145.16B	$505.11B	79%	
Belgium	$17.37B	$184.04B	$586.09	113%	
Bulgaria	$19.84B	$20.63B	$68.56B	25%	1980-2020
Croatia	$22.53B	$21.63B	$60.75B	86%	1985-2020
Cyprus	$0.49B	$5.59B	$24.95B	118%	
Czech Rep	$138.48B	$161.38B	$435.35B	30%	1995-2020
Denmark	$10.01B	$90.69B	$272.70B	42%	
Estonia	$8.89B	$12.61B	$48.63B	18%	1995-2020
Finland	$7.27B	$90.76B	$272.70B	69%	
France	$84.63B	1006.16B	$3101.77B	116%	
Germany	$154.08B	$1446.11B	$4542.67B	70%	
Greece	$9.59B	$137.56B	$323.10B	199%	
Hungary	$93.1B	$116.82B	$323.10B	81%	1995-2020
Ireland	$3.54B	$108.78B	$416.43B	59%	
Italy	$84.19B	$1510.88B	$2549.87B	156%	
Latvia	$13.73B	$18.40B	$61.28B	43%	1995-2020
Lithuania	$20.74B	$28.68B	$102.48B	47%	1995-2020
Luxembourg	$1.03B	$10.93B	$68.97B	22%	
Malta	$0.25B	$2.55B	$14.99B	43%	1970-2020
Netherlands	$26.06B	$277.72B	$989.54B	48%	
Poland	$284.34B	$397.06B	$1255.33B	57%	1995-2020
Portugal	$7.47B	$111.68B	$354.79B	130%	1987-2020
Romania	$38.41B	$37.25B	$250.68B	47%	1993-2020
Slovakia	$38.35B	$59.19B	$190.94B	60%	1995-2020
Slovenia	$26.67B	$34.87B	$82.04B	81%	
Spain	$34.48B	$511.26B	$1937.04B	114%	
Sweden	$17.32B	$167.64B	$549.99B	38%	

EU Figures pulled from www.europa.eu/european-union

Figures depict national trend toward Debt Increase and weight burden within the union. Lower GDP-to-Debt ratio nations are required to support debt-heavy nations underwater. Debt bonds and burden upon financial institutions to lend through international, but EU-Based nations, is required for sustainability of the union. Friction is felt as debt is spun out of proportion to GDP.

Central American Free Trade Agreement (CAFTA)

CAFTA, referred to as the Central American Free Trade Agreement, employs a NAFTA style governing authority over market parameters but just a bit further south. Unlike NAFTA, the Central American agreement weighs its bets heavily on light competitors. Countries involved include Guatemala, El Salvador, Honduras, Costa Rica, Nicaragua, and the featherweight contender, the Dominican Republic. Before we get into logistic diagnostics of faults and positive attributes, let's set the ring just a bit more.

We talked of proxy in conflict as proctors reign in shadow authority over another as an internal force cloaked as internal influence. The genetic code of an entity, such as France, Belgium, or Britain in Africa, is similar here in composition makeup as an agreement forms. CAFTA, and other treaties, are entities within themselves that act to manipulate the construct toward one understood and agreed upon common goal. The difference is interpretation and ability to manipulate the fine print. Just like any nutrient label on a box or bottle, no one understands the chemical makeup that lies within until they have explosive diarrhea or something worse, a prolonged illness undiagnosable to one specific consumption. Agreements, in general principle, are positive forces of bridges forming between one or more entities, ensuring collective progress toward a common goal. There are also agreements that cause one to "kiss their sister" in a sense. No one enjoys that.

You could even get into the Greek Oedipus Rex myth as a predestined path of inevitably for one to "kill their father and marry their mother." The environment in which an agreement is made is the same predestined existence of a story that foreshadows what's predetermined no matter how hard we try to deny inevitability. By fleeing so far, we find the edge of our paradox and act in which no action can deny the destiny of an ill-willed fate. An agreement, through genetically promising expansion of human rights and opportunity for Central American civilians will act only to which its proctor puppeteer is intrigued and encouraged to pull its puppet's strings. A promise between unaware and underlying preconditions predestines our relationship in agreement.

If you could bet against a fighter in a boxing match you know has a genetic disadvantage, wouldn't you if you profit? And then, is it fair then for that fighter to step in the ring unaware of status in conflict? Even if that fighter has a genetic disadvantage and everyone in the world knows except that individual? And then if the other superior fighter is incentivized to throw the fight? Then what is reality? A thrown fight is a win to an unaware and disadvantaged fighter. A thrown fight is then not a loss to the fight throwing fighter because external compensation legitimizes effort irrelevant to the actual perceived outcome. Who is what and when and where of CAFTA?

How is perception shaped in the world today? Depiction and manipulation of what reality is through senses that shape what we feel and think. Unaware of our conditional programming, this remains and the effect with it. Whether cognitive or not, every stimulant creates a response. Whether the commercial you are watching during your favorite show knows it or not, chemical changes are made with each musical note or change in light and darkness on the screen. Some, more than others, notice what is what. It is not to say deliberateness exists, but that effect does. Cause or not, irrelevant. How then can we again shape this agreement of lightweight competitors? Well, advantage through human nature is to capitalize advantage at the aware or unaware expense of another when the moment calls for individual optimization. This is whether the collective mutually benefits or is included or not. The perspective of each fighter, broadcaster, announcer, bookie and better is then manipulated looking at the same main event through different lenses with different measures of intent and actionable control.

The Ring and the Lights

In an isolated series of events, imagine a timeline of fights is scheduled to which a number of bettors book odds with a bookie. We have a bureaucracy of compartmentalized beneficiaries in this theater of entertainment. We have the bookie and bettor, we have the broadcaster, and we have the fighters. Bookies are those that leverage odds and bets. Broadcasters have the ability to show true, full, or incomplete coverage of fighters. Fighters then are the prop and strung out with a carrot of compensation in front of them even if the residual loss is physical harm or humiliation. The ropes of the ring outline the borders between where only two fighters are able to enter the ring at a time. Just as a bridge exists in our effort for cohesion and maintenance of coherent relationships based on reason toward a common goal, conflict can be presented inversely through the same application.

Imagine proxy economic conflict instead of physical altercations of rockets and armed brigades. Our example of economic proxy war is not necessarily as immediately threatening the life of another, but that exists not too far away. This is the middle ground between cohesive unification under one goal and complete and all-out war or conflict through proctor and proxy. Benefit through resource control exists shadowed just the same as one nation invading the continent of Africa for diamonds or uranium. Instead, we do it with suits and ties and the twist of reality through deceptive means. You may then notice the direction we are going here. CAFTA is no good. Between the beneficial weight of NAFTA and the EU as agreements for the common good, CAFTA is at the bottom of the totem pole. Let us look at our fighters, bookies, bettors and broadcasters, and *let's get ready to rumble.*

The announcer calls: *Welcome to fight night live from Las Vegas. Get your bets in. In the Blue Corner, we have Nicaragua standing at 5 foot 10 inches tall, weighing in at 145 pounds. In the Red Corner, we have Costa Rica standing 5 foot 9 inches tall, weighing 144.5 pounds. Stay tuned; the United States will be back live in 10 minutes for the beginning of round one.*

The key component of our measurement here, is the rate at which a proctor is aware of the proxying of a nation. We should look into everything from presidential legacy to standard party politics when forming the agreement in place. Tariffs were phased out for US imports into CAFTA nations last year after the agreement was signed in 2005. Just as we balanced a logic equation in *Volume 2*, we should here as well in very simple terms. The difficulty in this measurement is that logic is a process of reasoning to which we ourselves are unaware of the rate of cognitive awareness of either party. We can look for clues in historical context, but clues only will not paint the entire picture. We cannot speak to George Bush and ask because we are small people. We can guess and hypothesize and almost assume, which I do not like doing, based on other historical traits aligned with party intent.

Conservatism, whether cognitively aware or causally impaired, acts to conserve the individual over the collective. CAFTA is a very liberal application of conservatism in generalizing generic trade into one approach for the shadow benefit of the collective. The oddity, in that sentence, is when agreements are made by powerful nations with the illusion spun upon underdeveloped countries. The truth is in the tariffs and effect placed upon their removal.

After hesitant Central American nations signed and implemented CAFTA, tariffs were eliminated, and others began to phase out. Most phase-outs include agricultural industry-based products as the United States imports into CAFTA nations. Actual figures are depicted in a few paragraphs below to see the trade balance between nations before 2005, after 2005, and into 2020 with a measuring point in the middle.

The United States began to import relatively less from CAFTA nations and export more goods than ever. While US exports increased, the oddity is in how CAFTA exports into the US stood still. On both sides of cause and effect, we can look at the macroeconomics of this see-saw of who benefits and who feels the residual. Goods are sold cheaper as they enter CAFTA nations. Cause and effect. Tariff taxation at each border pre-CAFTA protected small businesses in the region. That buffer was eliminated. Perhaps US agribusinesses do not see increased revenue per capita because import levels remain, but what could be the intent?

If smaller nations involved in trade are importing but not exporting to and from the US, who are they trading with to create balanced supply against demand? Themselves. Underdeveloped nations much further south than just the Mexico-US border cannot compete in a superpower's climate of trade. United States goods are imported, but nothing is balanced as an export. Costs associated with exporting CAFTA goods are not competitively aligned with United States demand. What then is intended as we mention? Simple involvement. Perhaps, the United States can influence through economic pressure aligned with an agreement that weighs relations between but not among.

Awareness again is our key. A hot topic and controversy aligned with adopting CAFTA are generic pharmaceuticals and the destruction of Central American market share in their own countries. Was this an intentional act or a residual cause of the genetic formation and fine print in a document that now reigns over trade to and from? In a boxing match is this a bookie adding weight to the gloves of a fighter? And then, what is the awareness of a proctor proxying a nation economically?

Generic pharmaceuticals are either suffocated through marketing channels or are challenged through US Pharma law in a foreign nation under the guise of one agreement. The cost for HIV/Aids, malaria, and other pharmaceuticals sky-rocket, and US Pharma corporations begin to control output. Life-saving and altering medications triple and quadruple overnight sold only by US exporters. How do you discredit a generic drug made at a low cost to the consumer? Use national law to question the validity of practice in a foreign nation to stir uncertainty and control market share to garner export control not only in CAFTA nations but from CAFTA nations to the rest of the world. Human beings are naturally advantageous. That is natural Darwinist law. Sometimes superpower doesn't mean the natural goodwill or abilities of Superman.

Like any international trade agreement, a powerful nation, or broadcaster, can pick and choose what they want to prioritize, or show on tv, in austere practice to enforce the law or any law. In all international agreements, the hardest things to ensure and enforce to another involved nation, especially one that is underdeveloped, are labor rights and adequate working conditions. Imagine a multi-dimensional uprising in which union leaders revolt against the political party of a semi-civilized and part barbaric nation that signed an agreement that threatens union representation. They simply are assassinated, and trials against an accuser are not brought about for years to come because of the claim that human rights laws and labor standards in the US "can't govern over trivial crimes in another nation." The hypocrisy is just this. A superpower can enforce Pharma law as it is written in CAFTA, but they can't enforce the demand for equal labor standards? Where then is the balance in, not trade, but logic found in the preceding sentence. If A is A and B is B, how can one say we cannot enforce A because of B if the same logic was used to find C previously or currently in time? Reason and logic are not sound in this application.

Here is the fight card weighing in through historically recorded residuals both correlated and indiscernible but assumed to hold a causal relationship in our series of highlighted events and boxing matches. Economic trade measurements are pre-2005, 2012, and 2020. Social measurements are scattered but should be thought of in the context of the economic timeline of trade:

Bookie – Agreement Enforcement and Governing Authority
Bettors – Agribusiness, CAFTA Political
Leaders, Pharma, and everyone else
Fighters – CAFTA Nation and Civilian Workforce
Broadcaster – United States Government

Through the figures presented we can see the balancing and inversion of surplus between CAFTA nations and the United States. In a three-round title bout to determine the heavyweight champion of Central America, we look at the year 2000. CAFTA individual government ideology and the civilian nations fight an even first round. Going into round two, the CAFTA government, as an authority figure, swaps gloves and adds lead weight to them. Bookie and the broadcaster know what happened between rounds, but the commercial break doesn't show the truth. In rounds two and three, civilian workers are beaten to a pulp. Depicting the world is a fair fight. Agribusiness, political leaders on both sides, and Pharma corporations weighed the outcome of leveraging their bet. Even if complete control of the outcome is not maintained, probability weight on one side of the scale ensures a winning bet. All others are left to chance if the truth is not broadcasted freely and fairly. What happens behind the scenes is something some are aware of and others are not. In a game holding a Nash Equilibrium, risk and the probability to payout ratio is not the same for every bettor.

Let Them Eat Loaves

If the truth of anything is ever found in its pure form, it is in the math behind reason. Sure, dealings of emotion and relationships between people are tough but not absent of raw science. You or I or anyone anywhere may have a tough time extrapolating quantifiable logic behind principle, but that does not invalidate its existence. Physics, geometry, and any form of procedural analysis interpret abstract thought into numerical form. One may think numbers do not dominate biology and chemical reactions that create emotion, but that is untrue. You can, however, count and measure endorphin reactions and serotonin levels. Everything in the universe has a number applied to it.

The sound decibel related to the vibrational pitch of the radio is measurable. The light magnitude and voltage of the lights in your house are quantifiable. The reaction time and relativistic measurement and movement of two or more cars on the highway use the laws of motion and math to determine the true/false state of a traffic jam. Whether we formulate every number of our analogous principles presented here, or onward, is irrelevant. Just as the universe is infinite but encapsulated, this is our goal here as well. I would be walking out into outer space on a bridge to nowhere if I were to sit here and write every number because that bridge moves at a rate faster than I can write and publish a book. I could still be writing the first paragraph to *Volume 1* if that were the goal.

Perhaps we do not articulate entity involvement and the raw data behind each international agreement directly, but we could with what is presented here. We do just enough in knowing there is always more. Below are the trade numbers from three relativistic points in time to depict the curvature in trade directly correlated with CAFTA's application. What we see most of all is what we should be looking for.

That is any change from one competitive position to another. From 2000 to 2012 to 2019, we measure imports and exports to and from the US and into individual CAFTA nations. Observably, we can see the change of before and after to know where we are going.

US exports into CAFTA nations all represented a trade deficit pre-CAFTA application except for the Dominican Republic, which is almost even. As CAFTA is acted upon, most trade balances are flipped. Not all, but the vast majority of the United States's trade into individual nations begins to trend in the same direction, equaling a trade surplus for the United States. We know all nations have other trading partners but let us isolate our scenario like this. If CAFTA nations have no other partner to trade with and a deficit is run year to year, how do you foot the bill? Meaning, imagine imports and exports from each relative position as a cost or expense for creating one single loaf of bread. If one nation sells that loaf of bread to another, sooner or later, income will reduce to debt above GDP without question. The reason being, no other production exists other than this one loaf of bread as an import. As that loaf of bread is broken up and consumed, energy is created by each nation to produce all together only half a loaf of bread to which they sell that half back to the initial bread selling nation.

This process continues as a developed bread-maker can efficiently bake and ship more loaves at a lower cost relative to the cost of the nation that will buy that loaf. You may think that is a strange thought because I thought the United States was taking advantage of low-cost labor. Good thought, but we are not talking about the cost of labor. We are talking about the equitable price of a product. Cost is important, but our selling price is more relevant in this scenario. Where we looked at cost and labor conditions advantageously used through NAFTA, we are looking at the opposite and inverse through a separate perception. Just like how our WVI in *Volume 2* looks at four different points, in time and space, as the perceptive measurement of dollar to equity and equity to dollar holding both positive and negative charges, this is similar.

In our measurable weight an agreement holds we can look similarly both up and down and from who and where. We can look at cost equity to price equity the same. Our cost is relatively perceptive to another's selling price, both inverse in viewpoint and charge. In NAFTA, we focused on cost and cost control and manipulation. Our bread analogy, of import and export balance, is who and what controls the price and supply and balance between and the effect placed by an arbitrary, but agreed upon, value. At this point in trade, we are also then looking at margin and surplus or deficit aligned with price per traded commodity. Where a loaf of bread is easily produced in the United States, it is not as easily produced in our closed CAFTA scenario of balance in trade. As the United States has a number of resources easily at our disposal such as flower, water, heat, and ovens, CAFTA nations do not. What is required for production are imported goods. What is required by the United States to create a loaf, in relative perspective to CAFTA nations, is nothing. Now apply this to billions of dollars in loaves of bread, or corn, rubber, medications, tools, and other exportable goods. If one barrier, tariffs, stands in the way of selling one loaf or two loaves, why not remove it if you can sell two for the price of one. In reality, pre-CAFTA, the United States is almost the one selling half a loaf and buying one almost unnecessarily.

CAFTA/US	Honduras	Nicaragua	Costa Rica	Dominican R	Guatemala	El Salvador	Total
Exports 2000	$2584.0	$380.1	$2460.3	$4472.8	$1900.7	$1780.2	$13578.10
Imports 2000	$3090.1	$588.4	$3538.6	$4383.3	$2607.5	$1933.0	$16140.9
Balance	($506.1)	($208.3)	($1078.3)	$89.5	($706.8)	($152.8)	($2562.8)
Efficiency	0.8362	0.6459	0.6952	1.0204	0.7289	0.9209	0.8079
Exports 2012	$5714.7	$1128.2	$7236.6	$6967.4	$5748.9	$3095.7	$29891.5
Imports 2012	$4647.8	$2748.0	$12046.1	$4370.4	$4491.4	$2587.6	$30891.30
Balance	$1066.9	($1619.8)	($4809.5)	$2597.0	$1257.5	$508.1	($999.80)
Efficience	1.2295	0.4105	0.6007	1.5943	1.2799	1.1964	1.0519
Change From	0.3933	-0.2354	-0.0945	0.5739	0.551	0.2755	0.2440
Exports 2019	$5439.8	$1652.0	$6219.1	$9194.2	$6810.8	$3369.1	$32685.00
Imports 2019	$4823.5	$3883.9	$5147.3	$5553.0	$3987.6	$2480.2	$25875.50
Balance	$616.3	($2232.0)	$1071.8	$3641.2	$2823.2	$888.9	$6809.40
Efficiency	1.1278	0.4254	1.2082	1.6557	1.7080	1.3584	1.24725
Change From	-0.1017	0.0149	0.6075	0.0614	0.4281	0.162	0.1954
S. America	2000	2001	2002	2005	2009	2012	2019
Exports	$59282.7	$58155.9	$51551.2	$72323.8	$109548.8	$183184.0	$161624.3
Imports	$73347.7	$67370.0	$69503.2	$122873.0	$108099.1	$171791.3	$108860.9
Balance	-$14065	-$9214.10	-$17952	-$50549.20	$1449.7	$11392.70	$52763.4

Table Figures pulled from www.census.gov/foreign-trade

Noted are major CAFTA trading partners' import and export balances with the United States before and after CAFTA. Efficiency balance index is a measure around 100% equal balance in trade. Volatility is suggested as trading partners approach equal balance in trade. Once trading partners exceed a margin of error, trading balances have one definite direction until a new agreement is made. We can see this in trends and "Change From" balancing index to the right between our 3 points of reference. As total $ in trade increases and the United States' trade surplus increases, the trend upward cools but is still definable in one direction. This is a direct result of CAFTA.

Most, but not all trade balances flip. Trends in South America overall, depicted at the bottom, show a very clear path of surplus trend upward following the peak trade imbalance of 2005, consequently when CAFTA is signed and adopted.

What is the solution? Balanced equity in authority leads to a balanced increase in both imports and exports. If I were to draw a quadratic, which you know I love quadratics, you would see a heavy curve toward export equity loss to CAFTA nations. You can even use the figures presented just above and see it for yourself. Yes, CAFTA nations benefit from free trade with the fact that production will increase through incoming accelerants. But, is the growth rate equitably equal? *Volume 9, Global Field State Zero*, will dive into a complete measurement of this balancing act. At this point, we are still setting the stage to weigh and draw an optimal global velocity into equilibrium.

The usefulness and optimal maintenance state, or lack thereof, of CAFTA can be explained through the symbolism of the Pathway to Prosperity into Central America. As an infrastructural plan, like building a bridge, the pathway to prosperity is the attempt to link Western Hemisphere nations through more than thought and political ideology but in building roads for economic production to freely travel back and forth with the promise that prosperity will follow. The odd thing, there are always questionable living conditions close to major highways but the collective gains. Questioned though is, does the individual gain equity status? That is my question for you. In our symbolism of a bridge and the pathway to prosperity as an act and effort, it still remains a work in progress without measurable improvement. Spinning time and energy and input, more, hypothetically, should have been accomplished. The difficulty again, separate laws governing different lands for prosperity to traverse over and through.

As the support beams of our bridges and expansion conditions and suspension wires are formed, so can we form a similar model as the foundation of our hourglass. Through trade, not too much diverges from this principle. We are exchanging cost and expense through a hierarchical class structure as a link between two separate forms. The way in which we look at our model can add additional dimensions or shape them similar to previous diagrams. Our prismatic model and torus from *Volume 2* are depicted continuously in our analogy, but we do not draw it here. In all explanations, we describe the fluid dynamics between, in common language. If we were to draw the involvement of this agreement, what do you think it would look like? There are a few options. Industry type and economic components ensure cohesion by simply existing in a form that would shape any and all agreements. The question is, how many arms and legs? Or, how many hourglasses are connected, and at which point? As many as you want, depending on how you want to look at the weight in a relationship and what the goal of an agreement is. In a more dynamically unstable example, we'll look at this modeling through the looking glass on the Asian Pacific Partnership.

Asian Pacific Partnership

If we were to lay a framework for a future volume, it would be one in which we look at all molecular components and bonds between. In partnership, our goal is then one where balance is maintained over time. Is our bond to mesh forms into one or remain separate as we link entities at synapse ports and receptor points? As we looked into the process of merging forces during civil war conflict, what do we naturally see when space and time are converged by two forces sharing opposite charges? Massive friction where only one can remain. For this, the Pacific ocean is the only thing keeping the peace between nations. Imagine we take the country of China and pull it closer and closer to the western coastal beach against the Pacific. Where the shadowed figure in an ally-way holds questionable motives, a shadow is sometimes best because as we talk of awareness, sometimes what we do not know doesn't hurt us at the moment. The closer we get to an authoritarian nation in proximity, the brighter the light becomes, and the less a figure can hide in the shadows.

We know only a bit of truth about our trading partners across the pacific expanse. Obviously, those in the know understand the truth clearer of what happens on ground level. Tiananmen Square is one example, and light on humanitarian conditions civilians live under and willingness of a shadowed authority to do what is necessary, not to increase living conditions and standards, but maintain control. In trade, just as in any other relationship, we know who we are dealing with as if a first date is rude to the waiter but nice to us. Genetic deformity and malignancy are more present, ticking a time bomb of heat and friction that ultimately affects those within spatial proximity. Thankfully, again, the Pacific is a necessary barrier to separate superpowers.

Because we looked more into cause and effect on landscape maps and illustrations of the causal relationship between entities, we will dissect the Asian Pacific Partnership more literally and abstractly as our prismatic model form in the previous volume. Our effort in its entirety is equilibrium, whether in one entity or between two or more. Our prismatic fluid dynamic model from *Volume 2* is three-dimensional and depicts internal measurements against a hierarchy. What happens when we add another involved entity? We jump to the fourth. This, of course, is if we apply causal relationships between both internal forms while expressing the relationship between both models as external influencers. Meaning, we could maintain a three-dimensional structure to our measurement, but we can also add a fourth. Fun.

If we are to first draw a three-dimensional shape, we, of course, add spin and depth and pitch above and beyond the simple understanding and usefulness of dynamic polarity in both figure and form as applied. Time, and spinning the clock, allows us to see the manipulative perception of both internals against both externals. Imports and exports are depicted as external outlets or synapse points. Just as the thought of a mind, we then look at the emotion created or lacking through chemical exchange. Essentially, what happens to the body of one when the body of another feels an internal emotional response? We can see the radio broadcaster in our radio's hardware. If all things are connected in the balance of the universe, as we close and encapsulate an open system, an effect is made by the fourth-dimensional process between two separate entities. Tank Man affects the emotion of someone in Wichita, and our relationship externally through collective trade means can be measured similarly, symbolically, and synchronically through true, false, and inverted viewpoints. Tank Man, as a powerful symbol of the fight against totalitarianism, affects governmental forms of control in China but in the US as well. Internal to internal. Let's take a look and first lay the historical framework of not only trade but international relations too, from, across, and among nations of the Pacific.

Charting New Waters

Inverted perception is looking at the root cause followed by effect. In the United States this year, hate against those of Asian culture and descent is documented and has increased. The term "Go back to your country" is one that I have heard thrown around. Perhaps, stemming from COVID-19 and triggered in that way, animosity always finds a scapegoat. As we start to chart the water's, a perspective view is similar to the phrase used above. The oddity; China was an ally in World War II. Perhaps as an enemy to my enemy is my friend but still an ally. Similar to the theatre and actors in and of the Europe front at the time and specifically Russia as we remain at odds. The aligning difference, China is a massive trading partner. Without economic balance or dependability in mutuality, China would indeed be another Russia to us as a threat. But, imagine during World War II as the Doolittle Raiders parachuted into China if Chinese soldiers didn't say "Go back to your country" but said with malevolence, "You're in our country now."

This is the way in which viewpoints and perspectives are manipulated in time. Where China is now a trading partner but political adversary, Japan is both a partner in trade and ally for democracy. Causal, after World War II, we won't determine, but the change in perception is key. Atomically, perhaps enough polar charged accelerant, if we think in terms of ABi and involvement, engulfed a polar opposite charge to manipulate the genetic malignancy into goodwill even through a terrible act of violence. Yes, it ended the war and prevented mainland invasion. Thresholds and triggers exist in this sense. If, at one quick hot moment in time, a massive accelerant is charged against an entity in involvement that can sometimes invert the genetic charge of our mass, almost as if a defibrillator kickstarts a stalled heartbeat. Not healthy, but neither is dying.

There are a number of ways to look at a historical moment and what leads up to an event, and what happens in time even as that event takes place. There are a handful of scenarios, but if we broke it down, they would be just as the perspective of the internal populace as affected by time and space and our movement through both. Doolittle raiders dropping into China could have very well received the latter response of "You're in our country now" with either malevolence or goodwill. They could also receive the response of "Go back to your country" with both malevolence or goodwill. The fourth dimension exists in tone and interpretation and when fear and fight or flight is triggered or cooled by an ally's assistance and protection from harm.

Jumping through time, we arrive in 2005 with the implementation of an agreement between and among Australia, Canada, South Korea, India, Japan, and the United States. Even as CAFTA is signed around this time, the differences are clear in two forms: 1) The space between nations 2) Developmental status. All nations involved in this agreement are adequately equipped to produce and trade goods and services as some of the most elaborately built nations in the world. Infrastructure is adequate, but that does not mean diplomacy between, across, and to and from is.

The oddity in this agreement is that each nation holds proxies or proctors above or below them that don't see the world eye to eye with all other nations. China supports North Korea economically, not openly or publicly. In a way Russia does as well in some sense. South Korea and Japan, as closely proximal nations do not, and even feel the fury of North Korea's presence based in irrationality against the outside world. China also deals in proxy involvement with smaller southern pacific nations in Indonesia and the South China Sea. To which, within proximity, Australia trades outside the Asian Pacific Agreement. Canada is like, "Oh yeah, we like to trade. You trade, I trade." More of a passive approach, but, in response, work with nations in a lackadaisical but on mutually beneficial terms. This approach is very similar in Australia but with a slightly less laid-back tone almost only because of pent up anxiety just north in the China Sea that requires them to be alert. It is also tough to not be laid back when your main export is beef and not weaponry. I have yet to find a war fought over cows or with cows. India works with the United States as a close ally even if ideology or governmental structures are dissimilar. Common enemies have common friends, and those in the middle have a smile on their face but a motive in their mind.

The APP and RPEC, you can think of TPP (trans-pacific partnership) as well, are thrown into a melting pot in this section because they similarly aligned nations with both environmental and economic objectives and developed nations with two goals that intertwine even if space exists between. APP focuses on freeing communication to improve technologies of production to maintain a healthy global ecosystem. RPEC parallels trade between nations with the addition of New Zealand and subtraction of a rogue United States in 2017. Whether reasonable or not, the status is as it is with the United States's withdrawal. Collective cooperation is optimal when voluntary and not required by international law, and that is what APP forms in public to private incentivization to share environmentally sustainable production technologies as well as new energy-creating systems. Along the lines of other multinational trade agreements, RPEC does most of the same in cutting tariffs, defining intellectual property rights, and validating human rights and labor standards.

How we look at an agreement is less in what it says and more in the causal relationship between parties willing to be involved through the attempt of copacetic and cohesive means. Any non-agreement, whether trade exists or not, is reciprocal. Even if trade exists, and no agreement is signed for collective gain, adhesive fundamentals are found. The reason being, there is no acknowledgment of the effort for mutually beneficial trade. An act of trade in itself can indeed be cohesive in action, but the tendency is then to gravitate away. Effort toward equilibrium is to rectify an agreement equal in benefit and equitable in contribution. The way in which an agreement is made bonds each entity in involvement very similar to how a honeycomb is formed and measured and fundamental to a structural exchange of energy.

The B in Bond and Her Honeycomb

Volume 6, A Bond Unbound will focus on a very elaborate interpretation of what we discuss in this chapter and in the series of volumes to follow. Growing up in an 1800's Victorian house, we do not lack for books lost in time like treasures in the sand. One of my favorites to look through is titled the Bee and the Hive and analyzes how and why bees act. Sure, I am not a beekeeper, nor is my focus complete in understanding the importance of such a small creature to the sustainability of humanity, but because of this, I find the science incredibly intriguing.

When a hive is formed, the first thing worker bees do is form a network of hexagonal shapes to grow larva, sleep in and store pollen to create honey. If we are to look at this formation similar to the foundational structure of entity involvement, our goal is to create the same geometrical shape where each bee in the hierarchy of a hive holds certain responsibilities. We look at an agreement in trade, and the exchange of resources to form a cohesive bond, similar to the hive or whether our hives act adhesive against another hive.

Characteristics of the hive include different types of bees for different purposes. Of course, we have the queen, we have worker bees, and we have drone bees. Each in their own role, the queen, acts to populate the hive with new larva. Drones supply one end of the mating process with the queen and do nothing else really but eat and die. Worker bees are more numerous and essential to the hive's ability to thrive. The hierarchy of the hive is a closed system in that biological movement up and down is not allowed. Sure, we explained in *Volume 1*, wealth and value can move an individual up and down the latter. The absence of free will and cognitive ability to think outside this system and adapt as well as genetic makeup disallows this. Just as with the lion and the gazelle, movement is impossible. However, the difference is that our hierarchy is built for automotive cooperation to pollinate and create the sweetest possible honey.

Outside forces would include anything that threatens a hive's homeostasis or existence—a bear hungry for honey, killer wasps or murder hornets, and other invasive insects or environmental conditions. Bees are not equipped to fight off an attack other than the tactic to swarm and sting their attackers. This is useless against a bear and only more of a nuisance. Stingers are un-impactful against climate conditions. The fight against an army of wasps is then won only by numbers and sheer will to protect their queen.

Just as colonies of bees and hives allow for humanity to continue, so do a series of cohesively based agreements and treaties. The moment a treaty becomes applicable is the moment a wasp transforms genetically through a change in mass coding birthed into a new larva and not as a threat against the hive but as an attribute to colony survival.

You can think of this a number of different ways as well. A beehive in close proximity that does not invade another hive's territory to pollinate works copacetically but not cohesively. Just as what you don't know won't hurt you, sometimes what you don't know actually helps you. There are people that exist in this world that leave a ripple in your life, whether you or even them are aware. When someone smiles as you walk by them into the grocery store, as they are on their way out are those people. The ones that ask to take your grocery cart back for you as you leave and they are on the way in are the ones you are aware of. Sometimes you drive down the street or walk with your headphones in, and someone notices another driver is about to swerve into your lane so they honk. At this point, you don't know who or where it came from, but you act to avoid a collision and keep going. A series of hives act in this way for the positive common goal and survival of not only the human species but for themselves as well.

We could break a hive down into each and every person in the entire world. In a relativistic position with an accompanied measurement, an entity is either a drone bee, worker bee, queen bee, or an outside force in the shape of a wasp or a bear acting as a threat against the hive. From perceptible points of view, a bear can be both a bear and a bee, depending on who's eyes we are looking through. From North Korea's viewpoint, the United States is a bear or army of wasps where they act only with this belief. In reality, the law of averages in trade and conflict through history at any moment in time before, during, and since the Korean War places most perceptions against North Korea as the army of wasps led by a king wasp.

As an agreement is made, we begin to form our honeycomb and hexagonal shape between each growing larva, a drone bee that only consumes and dies or a worker bee that acts efficiently to produce more than they consume. In trade, which is what and where is which? If we are to look at CAFTA, at any singular moment in time, one juxtaposition can place either or any nation as a worker or drone. Pre-CAFTA, you could most comfortably place the United States in the worker bee category with the perception that individual CAFTA nations are relatively more drone-like in comparison. Post-CAFTA would flip the equation. If we weigh only the trade balance of surplus and measure an equity value in favor, we may place drone status upon the United States and worker bee status against all countries with a deficit working equitably more than their involved counterparts.

In the balancing act of market topography, what happens when there are too many drones and not enough workers? Consumption surpasses production, the hive dies. What happens when there are no drone bees and all worker bees? Production is higher than the ability to transform energy into life. The queen is left unable to reproduce larva. The hive dies. Do both sound familiar? This is the balancing act of the socioeconomic spectrum of pure socialism and pure capitalism. The same exists in market balance between involved entities in trade and weighing a deficit against a reciprocal surplus. All analogies aside, but parallel in orbital paths, how do we then look into the involvement of APP, RPEC, and TPP nations and measure the balance of our hive as an agreement is made, applied, and enforced? With ease.

The funny foreshadowing here is how we alluded to the benefit of humanity to produce clean energy as an agreement through APP and then the economic production behind RPEC. APP, in our hive and bee analogy, is whether our pollination continues or not in the sense the environment provides life for both vegetation to grow as well as prevent colony die-off. Economic agreements act parallel as a function to determine which bees go where and how and when a group of bees move to pollinate and feel the environmental effect or cost if pollination cannot continue. If there is too much carbon dioxide in the air and not clean oxygen, a cost is felt not immediately but inevitably. Our lungs hurt, we cough a bit, the planet warms, and ocean levels rise. APP then acts to benefit the hive to ensure worker bees have a resource to pull from and even share with other hives that act congruent but unaware and non-cohesive in trade. The removal of APP and the gravitation as far away from such a partnership is the death of the hive, both figuratively and realistically. The hive dies slowly with each worker bee that returns without pollen for the hive.

Twin Bee: Monozygotic and Dizygotic

When an agreement is formed, a genetic reaction occurs that forms the potential of one agreement between two entities. Just as siblings are born, and the biology of each, time affects the outcome. An agreement is the way two or more children are born at once, and the process of growth is aligned with genetic type. Are twins identical or fraternal? Monozygotic twins are genetically the same. Sure they may still be composed of slightly different strands of DNA, but are birthed from the same embryo. Fraternal twins only hold the same space in the womb and, by all definitions, are not identical. In this case, we have a few possibilities. Identical twins can be both boys or one boy and one girl. Fraternal twins have the same possibility. In this combination, irrelevant of gender, but dependent on fraternal or identical status, one may or may not be the same as the other.

Identical twins of separate genders can act both as worker bees. Fraternal twins can both act as worker bees only if they are both the same gender. We should summarize again, twin and gender type are only used as shared characteristics in combination, not definable variables only relativistic attributes. Gender and twin type are alluded to in comparison to the balance, in genetic coding at birth of an agreement between, of entity ideology or market type in governance. In our balancing act, when an agreement is made, identical twins will align with two characteristics and maintain cohesion naturally. Fraternal twins will align with one or none at all. Because time is static at the moment an agreement is made, and there is no separation between, the type of twins is important. Two of the same genetically formed siblings in agreement will align along all components within the agreement. Siblings that are fraternal will only share one or none. And yes, I know the term twin bee does not exist as I have not heard of bees being twins in any facet as one larva usually grows into one bee. Our hive, however in analogy, is a queen laying larva all at once, to which any involved entity is a twin, triplet, or more.

Let's then jump back into APP and economic partnerships. Japan aligns with the United States in both economic and environmental congruence. They are identical twins and of the same gender or not. I would say how we arrived at this point in history following World War II, the dimension would suggest one is a boy and one is a girl. The United States and China are fraternal twins. At any moment in time, this measure can change because we are free-willed beings and bees are not cognizant or able to change hierarchy status. For this, the United States is fraternal, and at one moment in time and with one trade, they can be matching genders. At any other moment, they could not be. Transformation is a property we rely on because we are cognizant. Or at least some of us.

Hexagonal Comb

The way our comb forms is the bond between multiple entities and imperative to the survival of the hive and for life to continue. How we link and interlock is important to align at each corner's edge. When a hive breaks down, it is the crumbling of each individual comb first before the entire hive collapses. As each bee that dies is not removed and replaced with new larva, the hive deteriorates. The way we describe our comb and shape can be looked at in a number of ways dependent on the makeup of the hive. An entity uninvolved with another is one hive with many workers. The moment we place a bureaucratic structure against a separate hive and link two or more in involvement is the moment two hives become one, and each entity moves from one hive as a whole into individual bees.

Dimensionally, a hexagon has six sides. Scientifically we can probably align this with the number of nations that are optimal for an agreement to work effectively for each entity. If the bee knows, the bee knows. Magic or science or the combination of both, probably true by assumption, imperativeness, and how a bee sustains all life through optimization in simplistic form. With bureaucracy involved then what is our goal? The symmetry of our shape asks for one thing and gives a few more: balance and strength are found—the unbalancing of our hexagon results in the loss of strength. Ideally then, six co-equal and equitable entities in both trade and resource management should form the first layer to which two can be attached and derive energy and strength from the center. At the center of our hive, we have the agreement that governs all actions. Juxtapositional to our main authority is then any sub-agreement which other worker layers can stack above and below. This is where perception is found as strength is displaced, rearranged, and lost only to bee-type in transformation but not when cohesiveness is added in agreement.

If we were to illustrate APP and RPEC, we would draw our main comb and begin to layer other combs linking heavier trading partners in proximal range. Where South Korea depends on the United States for both political and economic support, the United States will be placed positionally different, against or adjacent, in political and economic terms with China. As South Korea may rely economically on China, perhaps governments do not align to a comfortable corner as much as with the United States. Any link founded with solid bonds will create fluid energy through the hive as a whole, even if one connected link lacks.

So then, what are our six sides of our hexagonal shape? Well, we have three industries normally and three balancing forces that maintain homeostasis of one individual entity. If we were to flatten this prism, described in *Volume 2*, into one plane of view then we have six sides. Our dimensional shape and spinning central torus then becomes the inverted perception between entities we described previously. Every nation, at least those with the ability to formulate a multinational agreement, have all six traits and the ability to perceive partners looking from within as goods are both exported and imported. The perception is just that and understood in similar ways. Any export is an import to someone. Any import is an export to someone as well. Transactionally, every industry sector is somewhat involved, and the link between hexagonal corners of our honeycomb can then be linked more aligned with industry and not only an entity's edge; as external to external, external to internal, internal to external, and internal to internal causal relationships are formed and acted upon.

A balanced market has an equitable input to output system where all legs and arms are balanced to sustain autonomy from outside influence. Our effort in this model is to subjugate an outside force and cozy it up to a separate entity's edge for cohesion and transformation. In this way, we can still maintain autonomy as one singular entity or nation but apply balancing and involvement principles of all entities individually as a whole that's sum of parts manipulates the balance among but still between.

As we look at our illustrations and then jump to historical data to depict balance or imbalance, I want you to still think, always, of our bridge between. As sector edges meet at corners and link involved partners, the bridge remains but only as if each corner were a roundabout with one entry and two exit points.

A continuous path is linked to connect entity to entity where nations that produce and trade more in one sector than with other nations have priority passage. Perhaps if one nation is more dominant in agriculture than another nation dominant in the service sector, then each dominantly traded producer aligns with the necessary consumer. The thought again, this changes with every breath as well as with every product that is traded and every transaction that is made through time. For a bee, this happens with each mission to and from each territory of to-be pollinated flowers.

What is the perfect balance between and among all entities? One moment in time when equity is ideal and perfect among all nations through our bureaucratic layering of hexagonal shapes in our honeycomb. This would be hard to quantify but easy to illustrate because it is just as the honeycomb exists naturally. Perfect balance and the constant existence of the hive and thrive toward continued production is all that is asked. Sure, quantifiable measurements can and do depict the equilibrium of the hive. The irony is, bees are very good at symmetry.

The Coloring Bee

Everything happens from one singular point in space and time. One entity can become two or more through aligned collaboration toward a common goal. As agreements are made and shades of color are combined, our color wheel turns and spins. Depicted is this scenario in which our hexagon is formed. One nation holds all the colors of the wind until another joins and another and another in partnership toward this goal. What must occur is the separation along connected borders and bonds that a hexagon allows. As one nation dissolves, a separative model begins to form our shape from what was into what is.

Our spectrum sees three primary and three secondary colors. Just as industries in threes and supportive factions are a combination in relationship and involvement, three more are combined, with each relationship between two linked in secondary stirred hues. In involvement, color separation must be present to align with polarity. A heavier hue on one side of the spectrum non-aligned with the color across the wheel creates genetic imbalance. As we spin, our ideal scenario is any linking entities share reciprocally and balanced hues. If six nations are involved, then one of each color, both primary and secondary, are used. This does not mean one dominates Banking and the other dominates Agriculture, but an equal and equitable balance is present in all sectors. Sure, a hue can be slightly heavier in finance and the other in farming, but ideally, one weight equals the overweight of another. The figures below act to give you the idea that even if our book is again in black and white, the difference in shade should do well enough. Sometimes it is easier to see separation in color when you remove hue and only give shades of black and white. Perhaps we then notice we are missing a third important property in viewing the world where duality is not true reality.

The Hive is Five-Plus-One

There are three primary colors and three secondary colors. A hexagon has six sides. Perfect balance in symmetry through this spectrum and combined with the hexagonal shape is the color hue of six equally proficient factions or nations. A nation that holds 100% efficiency in governance but nothing else helps five separate nations that are 100% separately efficient in each Banking, Commerce, Agriculture, Services, and Manufacturing. The difference is each nation fails without the other. Perfect balance and symmetrical exchange in strength are found if one cannot stand alone. Obviously, nations achieve some sort of proficiency in a number of areas and some more than others in certain and specific areas. Optimal balance and dedication to an agreement would be a necessary reliability but adequate production in each of the six sectors is desired. There is one sector that I want you to think and wonder oddly about.

Commerce is not necessarily any one branch of industry nor faction of governance but the combination of governmental authority as well as banking systems and abilities of a nation. The trick in this question or noted characteristic is this is where an agreement links nations to nations through manipulative means. This is of course, manipulation, but in a good way. The laws of sovereign nations do not control banking nor governance of any separate entity or nation. Our agreement or partnerships in place as they are formalized manipulate this one genetic line of source code to match and pair nations together. If a bang created life, this is that merging action through fusion at one bonding point and fission at another.

The central point of any hive is what we mentioned prior. As the agreement coheres all entities involved together, this central hexagon is our queen and gives life and purpose to all other hexagonal ports and homes to worker and drone bees. Our central hexagon does not hold the genetic makeup of any one particular entity but all parts of commerce and control. A queen is not genetically physical in nature to defend itself but relies on all other bees to protect her as well as drone bees to add life to produce greater output in production.

The Queen B and Her Hive

Our queen is imperative to the hive's survival as life is drawn only from her. What then is the queen's responsibility to a hive that only involves one nation and not a combination of nations involved in a partnership or agreement? Our queen, in this sense, would be similar to not NAFTA, CAFTA, or APP but the Constitution of the United States of America. As a Queen is present, we then attribute our government as a monarchical republic to our vector state holding genetic code B in involvement.

Because in our *ABi* and *B ln*, we only measure involvement based on the existence of a separate nation or entity enacting pressured changes against our mass coding, we then only look at ourselves as B if no other entity is measured to imagine reciprocity. Our queen is our queen to which an oath of protection is given by every worker bee whether or not they turn drone. To concisely summarize the importance of the queen, it gives life to cohesive involvement. As the queen weakens or dies, adhesive principles tear cohesion apart, and a nation or group of nations involved in trade begin to separate where the struggle for life begins.

The figures below illustrate the structure of a comb as it becomes involved between entities. Because, as we describe, we include a separate outside force, we must abandon our prismatic model and add another dimension. Instead of a three-by-three shape, we must multiply our involvement model into a binary operation, replacing our singular and solely internal measurement model. A six-by-six structure combines each sector in exchange input to output energy as a change in one nation's sector affects a change in the other's. The condition of our bridge maintains this model until we add further dimensions of involvement.

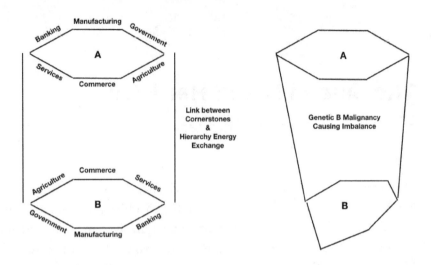

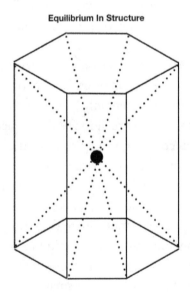

Equilibrium In Structure

The equilibrium state is the complete relativistic balance of all sectors' in equity related to trade and collective effort toward a common goal. At any one moment in time, optimization can be achieved as well as lost. With nations involved in trade that have varying levels of GDP and production rates as well as import and export variances, this does not mean only equally "rich" or "poor" nations can become balanced.

This also does not mean a trade deficit or surplus between exports and imports will create imbalance. This model means as trade between nations occurs, or the facilitation and implementation of one act in exchange for another, complete equitable trade is offered and afforded.

If our twin bees act unilaterally, our agreement and measure of involvement falters and becomes unbalanced. The moment a worker bee turns into a drone bee, consumption topples production output. Inversely, this can happen the other way, as mentioned. The way in which multinational agreements are made are then the placement in our comb in proximity and path to and from the queen. Let us look at how peace, or conflict, is tracked along the edge of each piece of our comb.

Peace by Piece Across the Pacific

Before we look into the real data of the Trans-Pacific relationship of a number of nations spanning the great Pacific expansion, or any other multinational partnership, we need to optimize our model. A hypothesis is written here in this volume for an experiment to occur in future measurement with a collection of data points. We know with certainty that perfect balance does not exist. We know, though as well, what perfect balance looks like. As we pair and bond nations around the central agreement, we know in which industry a charge must be added to a polar opposite relationship. We also know that as we formulate our measurement there may not be a perfect scenario, but there is a best-case with all variables in practice. Meaning, if South Korea and the United States pair relatively better in terms of trade of one good over the trade between nations over the same good, then this position should be a bond formed at a hexagonal corner. We know a hexagon has six sides of involvement to link nation to nation around one common goal, but we also know reciprocal trade the opposite direction between the same nations may be in a different sector. Meaning, if China is great at exporting steel and the United States is great at exporting agricultural products above and beyond any other nation, then this is the reciprocal link. As we draw metaphorical data points below and construct a honeycomb figure, think of this.

A quick question to note; What happens when one nation runs more deficit balances than surpluses in trade between countries and totals to a sum? Either they create massive amounts of internal energy through at-home production, are really good at propping up status by wealth creation or inflation control in substitution of legitimacy, or they hold firm by carrying a "big stick." With the hypothesis presented above, we can form our honeycomb below. Suppose we were a benign bear testing the sweetness of production. In that case, a satisfactory taste is attributed to a hive practicing balance and efficiency in pollen collection and transformation of input into perfectly sweet honey. As we described just previously in our queen B figure, inversion in relationships between bilaterally aligned agreements weighs trade through multiple perceptions. As one partner outweighs trade in one category but is more equal in another, not all stacks will align through involvement of more than two entities in agreement.

Stack A^1 can be to stack B^{-1}, but stack B^1 can be to stack C^{-1}, and C^1 to A^{-1}. This is where multidimensional reality in trade is seen. Below is a hive of some, not all, Asian Pacific partners in trade. What we discussed as well is that bureaucratic alignment allows stronger nations to surround the queen as both a wall of protection but also with the ability to facilitate relationships with smaller trade partners from the queen as our agreement is in play. This is solely a depiction in analogy to describe the way each hexagonal arm in our hive can both thrive but also deteriorate. Let's have a look.

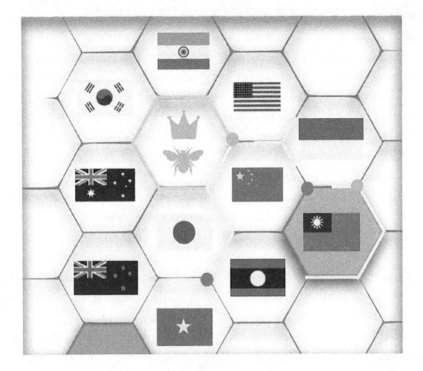

The queen is central to our agreement. Each hexagonal arm is a form of industry encompassing each entity. The difference between the queen's arms and the rest of the hive is that the queen is the "five in a hive plus one," meaning all efforts are to maintain an arbitrary variable as our agreement in commerce. Energy, carrying one arbitrary line of source code, is drawn from here for both consumption and production of all surrounding nations moving outward from the queen. In our figure, we draw how, and not necessarily why with firm figures or data. Data can be put to measure our comb's strength. Our goal is to think that this how can be applied before data weighs its test.

We also see how an export (green dot) can travel across and between and make it to a separate port. If our agreement, and the market aligned between and among nations, is cohesive in nature, each bridge between is strong, and passage can be made. Imagine if you will economic conflict between the US and China during a Trade War, and the South China Sea sees an increase in hostility. Further evidence space reduction is frictional tension only cooled by adding time between.

Laos, Taiwan, and some Indonesian islands are inhibited from transporting production to or from in a safe and mutually beneficial system of trade. For this, one arm of a hexagon is shortened to which bridge maintenance in agreement stalls our path then must be routed through space and time a different way. Where Laos may normally use the United States as an ally, and in times of peace in trade between China and the United States, Laos has no issue. The moment a trade war begins, China acts by proxy as a proctor and affects the ability of a trade partner of the United States to gain any advantage.

This then causes more energy against necessity. Where the path from one point to another is optimized by the fewest bridges crossed, the moment one port link of a cornerstone is destroyed, more edges and borders have to be traversed. Instead of traveling along two bridges now, we must cross three or four. Optimization is lost between Laos and other partners to which adhesive principles are applied to our system of trade around our queen, and the hive begins, in this static moment, to deteriorate. Any shrinkage in the link between edges is our bridge becoming unstable and support beams faltering.

The way we also link and measure placement of the hive is the relative position to which trade partners act in balance and strength in bondage. As we described, sometimes an exporter does not hold the same value as an importer and place one importer prioritized higher than another irrelevant of export capacity. If the United States is the number one importer of Chinese goods but the number three exporter into China, placement in juxtaposition is adjusted when polarity is altered through each transactional moment. In our measurement, perhaps for one moment in time or measurement within a year, the European Union exports a higher rate of goods and services into China, then they would hold our C^{-1} value to B^1 where the United States then links potentially with another nation. In our measurement of the comb in one separate agreement, where outside forces are externally non-linear with this trade partnership, the highest priority exporter in the batch of nations will align appropriately above a relatively lower-valued partner.

At Dawn, Let There be Light

Where energy is created, production is present. The measurements we have applied though question where that energy production is beneficial and benign or radioactive and residual. In continuing these excerpts and moving forward through our volumes, we apply this stage-setting idea into application. Measurement through quantifiable data is our goal even as our approach maintains theoretical in application. What we benefit from is the mold-ability of math to shape our understanding of the world. First, we need models and principle explanations to replace the darkness of unawareness and replace it with the light of an idea.

We have looked into conflicts in arms through internal and externally charged wars throughout history. The civil war in the United States to confrontations in Africa fueled by external proctors and then inability to suppress a large fire in the Middle East. Agreements in terms of economic policy and trade through diplomatic alliances aligned with similar fundamentals. Involvement is our key, and so is the simplicity between A and B. As we interpret the outside world, we do not think outside the box; we do not say a box does not exist but that we are aware of what we need to extrapolate and put into our box of measurements and transformative process of positive manipulative practice to reform reality to which we are differentiated from.

If we wanted to look at the United States and Russia, a similar measurement would be made. As the nation north of Europe annexes Crimea and becomes proctor over Ukraine, back and forth across border lines, throughout history, we can look through this same lens. If we wanted to measure cyber-attacks against political ideology in the United States from China or Russia, we could and the effect on the American psyche as it relates to choosing our own path. Proctors can be proxied as well through the process of Trojan thought and influence. Suppose we want to isolate North Korea in model and measure. In that case, we may align with a similar measurement of Iran, Iraq, and the ideological differences in the Middle East but add the intent that they have nothing we want. The continued measurement of Saudi Arabia and Iran, and India as a measurement that affects each nation tragically, we again would continue to look at the numbers. Economically we think in dollars and equity. Societally, in conflict, we think about the measurable separation or cohesion with ideology and the number of people harmed in confrontation. When all the dust settles, and all conflict and friction between parties is mitigated, the bridge between nations is formed, like iron ore heated and cooled once removed from the fire, by the connecting covalent bonds of both necessity and trivialities.

Cohesive principles, like the strands and entanglement of our own biology in DNA replication and translation, depict the process of a global society. We are all intertwined around the polarity of electrical charge. From different viewpoints, we experience the world and feel the change of emotion like a wind in our sails. It is always a matter of where we are going or where we are coming from as well as how long it takes to get to either point. Positive and negative values matched inversely with the combination of space and time act to process and create the light of our understanding, a spectrum that aligns with all things. As our mass object measurements can change, their space is altered. As they move through time, their effect is felt against another determinate of the relativistic space held and space between. Just as the moon and the sun share the Earth in Night and Day, balance is maintained even if some days are longer than others. We must only act to reduce the residual effect and fight the night in the shadowed heart of the Kraken to let mankind bask in the light of a new day.

Conclusion

As the world turns, our interpretation must turn with it. While one nation acts to burn bridges, another acts to mend relationships and create new links between, smelted steel from iron ore and carbon. Our effort in this volume is settled in the theoretical approach to paint a picture and then measure the figures within. The goal in any relationship, whether between two individuals, between two nations, or within the soul of the individual, is to maintain balance in polarity. As involvement becomes a gravitational force, causal effect places reactionary principles both to and from and up and down. The observable position or viewpoint of each perceiver is imperative to understand why we see the world as it is. Whether the protagonist of theater or a true victim of war, a reciprocal false state or antagonist remains a Kraken in the night growing deep below the surface of awareness.

Reality, however, is no more than the law of averages that act in balance or imbalance. Each individual as a sum to the whole acts against our regression model in both biological and interpreted processes. As a thought through history, from the caveman era to the Renaissance, that creates an emotional response is then the science between the radio and broadcaster's voice. Even though one cannot reach in and touch the source of output, we can look into the components that cause us to hear and interpret the frequency and vibrational sound that's outputted. Where a caveman would be shocked to hear a baseball game through a box, new age reality bends our understanding to make sense of what we hear, see, feel, touch, taste, and perceive. Our senses, in tune with nature and our ability to accept nurturement from environmental forces, build our understanding of what the universe, life, and reality are and can be.

One thought of new origin has its base somewhere in the vector of reality in both space and time. Chartered in open waters, or on a dimensional plane with intersection points and parallels upon axes, we measure the state to which our dynamic system rests positionally relative to equilibrium. At any moment in time, the genetic makeup of our socioeconomic system in homeostasis can be manipulated and pushed or pulled away by an adhesively concocted accelerant. Both act in a relativistic causal relationship. One action never lacks an opposite residual effect. Both internal and external forces will manipulate the genetic constructs through involution and evolution to either bring expansion endpoints closer together, or pull them further apart, in space or time.

Our bridge is just the result. As one entity clashes into another, genetic composition and makeup will determine the result. If space is added between, time can be reduced to act in a similar principle. If time is added between, space between is an asymmetrical variable. Whether this is in friction or in fusion or fission, our goal is for interaction to cause clean energy, not malignant radiation. While two nations act in conflict, they are maneuvering to burn the bridge between. The reciprocal state is agreement to which peace or production optimization is the point into infinity we chase where the measurement between is only but a singularly dense point. By maintaining balance in the expanse of space and time, we ensure every member of society as a migrant of one global nation, traveling both to and from, can safely traverse land over sea without the risk of nefarious malevolency; and make it to the *other side.*

CPSIA information can be obtained
at www.ICGtesting.com
Printed in the USA
BVHW081049030921
615950BV00002B/64

9 781637 285015